THE FRENCH COOK

Other books in The French Cook series:

Sauces

Cream Puffs & Éclairs

Soups and Stews (forthcoming)

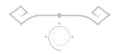

THE FRENCH COOK

SOUFFLÉS

GREG PATENT

Photographs by Kelly Gorham

GIBBS SMITH

TO ENRICH AND INSPIRE HUMANKIND

"The only thing that will make a soufflé fall
is if it knows you are afraid of it."

–James Beard

To Judith Weber, my agent, for her
unstinting support of my work.

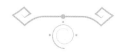

First Edition
14 15 16 17 18   5 4 3 2 1

Text © 2014 Greg Patent
Photographs © 2014 Kelly Gorham

Published by
Gibbs Smith
P.O. Box 667
Layton, Utah 84041

1.800.835.4993 orders
www.gibbs-smith.com

Designed by Sheryl Dickert
Page production by Renee Bond and Virginia Snow
Printed and bound in China

Gibbs Smith books are printed on either recycled, 100% post-consumer
waste, FSC-certified papers or on paper produced from sustainable PEFC-
certified forest/controlled wood source. Learn more at www.pefc.org.

Library of Congress Cataloging-in-Publication Data

Patent, Greg, 1939-
The French cook : soufflés / Greg Patent ; photographs by Kelly Gorham. — First edition.
    pages cm
Includes an index.
ISBN 978-1-4236-3612-0
1. Soufflés. I. Title. II. Title: Soufflés.
TX773.P355 2014
641.82—dc23
                                        2013037568

Contents

INTRODUCTION

I came to soufflés, or, rather, they came to me, through Julia Child. I had learned to cook and bake long before, through local television cooking shows in San Francisco, where I grew up during my second childhood. But soufflés never figured into my early self-training.

Enter Julia, who made all sorts of soufflés on her black-and-white TV series, *The French Chef.* I watched every week with my wife and scribbled down the recipes in my notebook. In the week between shows, I made what Julia made, and that is how I truly learned the fundamentals of cooking.

Baking is another story. I developed my love of that while living with my Iraqi grandmother, Granny, in wartime Shanghai during World War II, during my first childhood. The things she pulled out of her tiny oven were utterly amazing. And perhaps the most amazing of all were her sponge cakes: light, high, tender, delicious—always. I'd watch as she poured egg whites onto a ceramic platter and whipped them into billowy clouds with a fork! At the time I didn't realize the awesomeness of that task. But if necessity is the mother of invention, Granny was it.

I started baking at the age of eleven, when we immigrated to San Francisco. Television was in its infancy then, but major cities all over the country broadcast local cooking shows. By the time I was eighteen, I entered the 10th Pillsbury Bake-Off and won second prize in the junior division for my Apricot Dessert Bars. Baking was in my blood and I baked as much as I could, staying at home after school to tinker in the kitchen instead of going out to play.

When I watched Julia making her first soufflé, I immediately thought of Granny and how she whipped her egg whites. Julia used a copper bowl and a huge whisk and had the job done in short order. In other shows she'd use an electric mixer, which really didn't save any time at all.

What I learned from Julia were the basics of making soufflés. A soufflé has two parts: a base, which carries all the flavor and must be seasoned strongly, and the whipped egg whites, which must be beaten correctly and incorporated into the base gently to maintain as much of the air whipped into them as possible. Why? Because it's the whites that are the active part of a soufflé, causing it to rise. And, in French, *soufflé* means "puffed up."

Julia always stressed the importance of using grease-free utensils when beating egg whites because fat inhibits the process. I learned why many years later when scientists explained it. And every time Julia made a soufflé, she showed how to incorporate the whites into the base correctly by "folding" them in for maximum retention of air.

My first soufflé, following a Julia recipe, was the classic French cheese dish *soufflé au fromage*. It rose so high it reached the top element in my oven. Of course, I was hooked, and went on a soufflé binge, making all sorts of savory and dessert soufflés.

Years later when we traveled to Europe on the *S.S. France* with our two young boys, we were fed haute cuisine French food every lunch and dinner during the five-day crossing. In Paris I was thrilled to find a copper bowl and giant whisk, exactly like what Julia used on her show, and bought them on the spot.

What intrigues me most about soufflés is the power of air in causing these miracles of the kitchen to rise. The heat of the oven expands the tiny bubbles beaten into the whites to such a degree that a soufflé can almost double in size. And that's what makes it so light and tender.

Soufflés go way back in history, a French invention of the late-eighteenth century. The art of making soufflés wasn't codified until the 1820s, when Chef Antonin Carême described it in great detail. By then, the airflow in an oven could be controlled via the flue, allowing the cook to gain much better control over the oven's temperature. A soufflé depends upon a steady temperature for it to rise successfully.

Carême baked his soufflés in straight-sided stiff pastry casings that were not eaten.

And their straight sides carried over to the design of today's ceramic and metal molds. **Ceramic molds** today have ribbed sides. They are glazed on the inside and the sides but left unglazed on the bottom. Madeleine Kamman says, "The striations, together with the perfectly straight sides of the dish, ensure even penetration of the heat through the entire batter" (Madeleine Kamman, *The New Making of a Cook: The Art, Techniques, and Science of Good Cooking*. New York: William Morrow, 1997).

As with all cooking, using **top-quality ingredients** will produce the best soufflés. If flavoring with liqueurs, use only the best ones. Vanilla extract should be pure. Seek out the finest cheeses, chocolate and cocoa. And use organic butter, flour, dairy, and eggs if available.

With today's modern kitchen equipment, making a soufflé takes little time and produces spectacular results. One thing to remember about soufflés, however, is that you must wait for them; they won't wait for you. A soufflé retains its puff for only a few minutes after it's out of the oven and should be eaten as soon as possible. There's a story about the great French chef Auguste Escoffier and how he managed to have a dessert soufflé ready at exactly the right time for a fancy dinner. Because the dinner was an elaborate affair of many courses and also various speeches made it impossible to time the dessert exactly, Escoffier and his staff made ten different batches of soufflés three minutes apart to assure that one would be ready at just the right time. The rest were thrown out.

In this book, I teach soufflé basics and also some embellishments. Any cook with an understanding of a few soufflé basics can make a soufflé to be proud of. So let us begin.

Soufflé Basics

A Lesson on Eggs

We already know that a soufflé is a light and airy, highly flavored baked dish with a creamy texture. It can be savory or sweet. Soufflés may be baked in individual ramekins or in large molds, and in some cases, such as a fallen chocolate soufflé cake, deliberately allowed to fall and served cold.

A soufflé is created in two parts: a base and beaten egg whites. There are several bases available to the cook: a *béchamel* (a cooked flour-based sauce containing milk and egg yolks); a *velouté* (the same flour-based sauce with egg yolks but made with a liquid other than milk), a *bouillie* (a thick flour-and-milk paste boiled and beaten with butter, egg yolks and flavorings), or simply a fruit or vegetable *purée base* with or without egg yolks.

Proper handling of the egg whites, which causes the soufflé to rise, will guarantee a soufflé you can be proud of!

Separating whites from yolks

The first step in making a soufflé is to separate the whites from the yolks. Use cold eggs at this stage because there is less chance the yolk membrane will break when cold.

There are a number of ways to separate eggs. The traditional method uses three bowls. The rim of the first bowl should be thin so that when you crack the egg against it, the break in the shell will be clean. Separate the two halves of the shell and pass the yolk from one half of the shell to the other, allowing the white to drop into the first bowl. If the yolk is intact and the white is pure, put the intact yolk into the second bowl and transfer the white to a measuring cup or other container. The third bowl is there in case of an accident. Sometimes the yolk breaks when you crack the egg and contaminates the white. In that case, drop the whole egg into the third bowl and save it for another use. Sometimes, if there's only a little yolk floating within the white, you can remove it with a spoon and still use that white.

The way of many professional chefs is to crack the egg on a countertop and break the egg into a bowl. The yolk is lifted out with a clean hand and placed into another bowl. The egg white is moved to a measuring cup or other bowl. Cracking the egg on a flat surface minimizes sharp shell fragments that can break the yolk and cause contamination of the white.

Why no trace of yolks in the whites?

Egg whites are made of protein and water. You can see right through a raw egg white because the protein units are separate and allow light to pass between them. When beaten or heated, the bonds that hold the protein units together break; the proteins unwind and change in shape, and the proteins become *denatured*. These denatured proteins link to each other and form a three-dimensional meshwork. As beating creates

more and more of these denatured proteins, the meshwork gets larger and larger, trapping air in bubbles of protein and causing the whites to increase in volume. As this happens, the large number of proteins linking together no longer lets light pass through and the whites become opaque.

Egg yolks contain fat in addition to protein. If fats are beaten with whites, they prevent the egg white proteins from linking together by interfering with their bonding. A small amount of fat will still allow some of the proteins to hook up, but the amount of the meshwork formed will be lessened, and there'll be a corresponding drop in the volume of the beaten whites. Thus it is essential to beat whites in a clean bowl with a clean whisk.

Does the freshness of the egg matter in soufflés?

Some chefs swear by old egg whites—even weeks old—for making soufflés. Old whites are thin and will whip up faster and easier than gloppy fresh egg whites. They also mount up to a greater volume than fresh, I'm told. However, fresh egg whites make more stable foam, which is highly desirable in a meringue or cake. Frozen egg whites—the ones you freeze yourself—are excellent to use in soufflés and cakes. I've kept whites frozen for as long as one year in heavy-duty zip-top bags and they work extremely well in any soufflé or cake that I make.

I tend not to fret over the freshness of egg whites in making a soufflé. I buy fresh eggs at farmers markets and refrigerate them, and they're always waiting for me for whatever baking I may be doing.

Is temperature of the whites important when beating?

For maximum volume, egg whites should be beaten at a cool room temperature. Separate the eggs when cold for best results, then allow the whites to come to room temperature before beating them, because warmed whites denature more rapidly than cold ones. If you're in a hurry, set a bowl containing the egg whites into a pan with hot water and swirl the whites in the bowl for a few seconds to take the chill off. Now they're ready to be beaten.

To salt or not to salt?

During many years of baking, every time I came across a recipe for beaten whites, the instruction said to add a small amount of salt. Then research showed that salt decreases the stability of egg white foams, causing them to lose moisture and become dry. What to do? For flavor, I still add the pinch of salt called for in most soufflé recipes, and the mechanical effect on the whites of that small amount is not worth worrying about.

The stabilizing effect of sugar

If you overbeat egg whites, the denatured proteins squeeze together so tightly that they force out all the water trapped in the meshwork. The whites become lumpy and hard and impossible to work with. Non-dessert soufflés don't contain sugar, so it's important to beat the whites only until they form stiff peaks that hold a point and no further. Dessert soufflé recipes call for adding sugar to egg whites. Why? Aside from sweetness, sugar adds stability to egg whites by providing a syrupy coating on their denatured proteins. The coated proteins

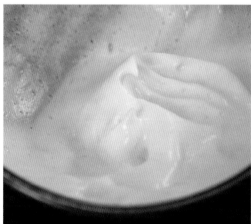

in the meshwork can't join with each other to squeeze out the water, thereby protecting the whites from collapsing.

When are the whites beaten enough?

This is the most pertinent question because soufflés rise solely due to air beaten into the whites. Properly beaten whites increase by seven to eight times their original volume. One large egg white measures about 2 tablespoons. Seven times that equals almost 1 cup.

For savory soufflés, which lack sugar to strengthen the whites, keep a watchful eye on the whites as you beat them. If you beat by hand with a wire whisk, it's rare to overbeat the whites because you can stop often to see how the whites are behaving. *When the whites cling to the wires, are shiny, and form peaks that hold a point when the beater is lifted up from the beating bowl, the whites are ready.* An old recommendation I read years ago said to beat the whites until they wouldn't slide in the bowl when you tipped the bowl from side to side. But it's better to stop just before this point.

When beating with an electric mixer, it's easy to overbeat the whites, so be vigilant. Start beating the whites with a pinch of salt (if using) on medium speed until frothy, about 1 minute. Add the cream of tartar and continue beating another minute or so, until the whites form soft mounds with droopy peaks when the beater is raised—the soft-peak stage. If making a savory soufflé, detach the beater from the machine and, holding it with your hand, finish whipping the whites until they form firm peaks that hold a point. If making a dessert soufflé, once the whites have reached the soft-peak stage, add the sugar a tablespoon at a time while beating on medium speed. Wait a few seconds between additions. When all of the sugar has been added, increase the speed to medium-high and beat not much longer, until the whites form stiff, shiny peaks that curl slightly at their tips when the beater is raised. You can also complete the beating by hand if you wish.

The more you practice beating egg whites, the more proficient you'll become. In fact, I encourage you to practice by separating a dozen eggs and beating up the whites in four batches—two savory and two sweet—to get the feel of how to handle egg whites. You can turn the egg yolks into a couple of batches of Crème Anglaise (page 114).

Beating yolks and forming the ribbon

Most soufflé recipes—both savory and sweet—say to whisk unbeaten yolks into the soufflé base. No problem there. Add them one at a time to the base and whisk after each until thoroughly incorporated. Sometimes I read a recipe that says to "beat the yolks until thick and pale" or "thick and lemon colored." But these directions don't say *how thick* the yolks should be. A more proper instruction is to "beat the yolks until they form the ribbon" or "beat until the yolks form a slowly dissolving ribbon when the beater is raised." Now, what does this all mean?

When you beat yolks with a whisk or electric mixer for several minutes, with or without sugar, they thicken, increase in volume, and turn pale yellow. After turning off the mixer and raising the beater a few inches above the beaten yolks, the thick yolk clinging to the wires of the beater falls onto the yolks in the

The ribbon.

bowl in a strip that's called the "ribbon." If you move the beater as the yolk falls from it, you'll see the ribbon sits on the yolk in the bowl for a few seconds then slowly dissolves into it. At this point, the yolks are beaten enough and you can proceed with the recipe.

Folding

Once you've made your base and beaten the whites properly, the two need to be combined with the goal of preserving as much of the air in the whites as possible. Folding accomplishes this. It is a way of getting the heavier base to accept the lighter whites. Sometimes, before you can begin folding, a recipe will say to actually stir or whisk some of the beaten whites into the base to loosen its texture and make it more hospitable to being combined with the remaining whites. In this case, some of the whites are sacrificed to assure the rest of the whites can combine easily with the base and retain the maximum amount of air.

Folding takes longer to describe than to actually do. When folding, scoop some of the beaten whites on top of the base in your mixing bowl or saucepan. Light mixtures go on top of heavy ones and not the reverse, because heavy bases can deflate beaten egg whites if placed on top of them.

Use a large flat-bladed rubber (or polycarbonate) spatula 4½ inches long and 2½ inches wide, and preferably with a rounded edge. Position it at the edge of the bowl's center. Cut down through the whites and soufflé base as you drag the blade towards you to the opposite side of the bowl. As you do, turn the

Scoop whites on top of base.

Cut down through whites and base, then drag spatula blade towards you.

Bring spatula up over the surface.

Repeat until combined.

spatula blade and bring it up along the side of the bowl, flipping it upwards and over the surface of the whites in the center of the bowl, carrying some of the base from the bottom of the bowl. Turn the bowl a quarter turn and repeat the motion over and over. Work rapidly, turning the bowl with each folding motion, until the base and whites are thoroughly combined. If a few streaks of white remain, just leave them alone. Once you get the hang of it, folding takes less than a minute. Now you're ready to put the soufflé batter into individual ramekins or one big soufflé dish.

EQUIPMENT

Saucepans, whisks, spatulas, wooden spoons, electric mixers, and mixing bowls are pieces of kitchenware you're likely to have on hand. A copper bowl (should you want to use one), soufflé ramekins, and larger molds are pieces you may want to acquire, as they will increase your enjoyment of making soufflés.

Saucepans: The three-quart size is most useful because it can hold the soufflé base and the folded-in beaten whites to complete the recipe. A one-quart saucepan is handy for heating liquids to add to a sauce base, and a two-quart saucepan is excellent for making Crème Anglaise, Lemon Curd, Raspberry Coulis and other sauces.

Be sure the saucepans are nonreactive, meaning they won't react with acidic ingredients and cause discoloration of a sauce or discoloration or pitting of the pan. Any citrus juice, wine, certain vegetables, and a few other ingredients are acidic. Stainless steel, enameled cast iron, and anodized (not plain) aluminum are all nonreactive. Well-made nonreactive pans will last you a lifetime and are worth their expense.

Whisks: You'll reach for medium-size whisks, about 10 to 12 inches long with wire heads 2 to 3 inches wide, most often when making soufflés, so have two or three of them. A small

whisk, 6 to 7 inches long with a wire head about 2 inches wide, is very useful for combining small amounts of ingredients. Look for whisks with many wires because they do the best job.

For beating whites by hand, a really large whisk, about 20 inches long with a wire head 4 to 5 inches wide, is great. Especially for beating by hand, use a whisk with many looping wires. The bigger the whisk and the more wires, the faster the whites will whip up to an impressive volume.

Spatulas and spoons: These can be made of heatproof silicone or wood or nylon. When making a cooked soufflé base, wooden or nylon spoons are the perfect tools for making the roux—or cooked butter and flour base—before adding a hot liquid such as milk or stock. Spatulas come in handy for scraping the bottom and sides of the pan as the base boils, particularly where the sides and pan bottom meet. Whisks come into play in a cooked base to help keep it smooth.

Electric mixers: A hand-held or stand mixer really speeds up whipping yolks or whites. Stand mixers are equipped with a large wire whip that does a splendid job of whipping air into egg whites. I've been using a KitchenAid mixer—the same one—for over forty years. The beater constantly moves about the bowl, insuring maximum incorporation of air into the whites. If using a hand-held electric mixer, choose one equipped with beaters that have slender wires, and be sure to move it all around the bowl as you beat to incorporate as much air as possible. Also use a hand-held mixer to beat yolks to "the ribbon" (see page 16). Hand-held mixers work perfectly well if a recipe calls for only a few whites and no yolks, and also for Crème Chantilly (page 115).

Mixing bowls: Stainless steel or glass bowls are the best choices. You will want small, medium, and large sizes. Avoid beating egg whites in a plastic bowl or with a plastic whisk. Fats cling to plastic like you wouldn't believe, and I've never had success beating whites in such bowls.

Copper bowl: French chefs and many home cooks use an unlined copper bowl for beating eggs whites, with or without sugar. A copper bowl works extremely well because the metal binds to an egg white protein called conalbumin (also known as ovotransferrin), producing a very stable egg white foam. A silver bowl works well, too. Lacking these, cream of tartar—an acidic powder (tartaric acid) derived from wine fermentation—stabilizes egg white foams very well and allows beaten whites to maintain their volume for several minutes. You need only a small amount of cream of tartar, and it really helps the whites hold a point and not separate into a watery layer.

If you want to use a copper bowl, get one about 10 inches across; probably expensive but worth it, in my opinion.

To clean a copper bowl, rub the beating surface with 1/4 cup distilled white vinegar and a tablespoon of salt. Rinse well under running tap water, and dry with paper towels. Don't use soap and water to clean a copper bowl.

Soufflé Dishes: I like serving appetizer and dessert soufflés in individual *ramekins*. I prefer main dish soufflés in one large 6- to 8-cup *mold* or in an oval or round glass or ceramic mold with a 2¹/₂-quart capacity. A 6-ounce ramekin is ideal for most hot dessert soufflés. For frozen soufflés, which generally are richer, I prefer 4- to 5-ounce ramekins. Some hot dessert soufflés, especially chocolate, need to be baked in 8-ounce ramekins. If you have six to eight of the 4-, 6-, and 8-ounce sizes and one each of the 6-cup and 8-cup molds, you'll be well set. For the latter, consider buying classic charlotte molds made of tin, with small heart-shaped handles. Their 4-inch-high sides give soufflés great support.

I've always used soufflé dishes made in France: Emile Henry, Pillivuyt, Apilco and Rovel are brands I can recommend.

When making soufflés, you have lots of options for *other baking molds* in addition to the traditional ones. Coffee mugs, glass custard cups, teacups, and just about any ovenproof straight-sided or flared vessel will work. Layer cake pans or pie plates, for example, would work for shallow soufflés. A Pyrex 2-quart measure is a great substitute for an 8-cup soufflé mold.

PREPARATIONS FOR MAKING SOUFFLÉS

Before you start making a soufflé, it's a good idea to decide on the dish you're going to use and prepare it to receive the batter.

Preparing the soufflé molds

For dessert soufflés, spread softened unsalted butter with your fingertips—about ¹/₂ teaspoon for each ramekin—to coat the inside of the ramekin all the way up to and including the rim. Repeat with remaining ramekins. Add about 3 tablespoons granulated sugar to a ramekin and turn it around to coat the bottom and sides. Dump the sugar out into the next ramekin and repeat until all the ramekins are coated with sugar. The procedure is the same if making one large soufflé. Once the molds are coated, refrigerate to set the coating.

For savory soufflés, butter the soufflé dish(es)—which may be a pie plate, a serving platter, individual ramekins, a large soufflé dish, or an au gratin dish—and coat with what the recipe calls for, usually cheese, bread crumbs, or flour.

Can you use a vegetable oil spray? Theoretically, yes. The sugar crusts nicely but only if very little spray is applied. Too much and the sugar has an unpleasant granular feel. Of course, there would be no butter flavor, which is an important part of the soufflé-eating experience. The flavor of the oil in spray cans is not very appealing. Whereas butter interacts with the sugar to produce a delicious layer of buttery crustiness, the vegetable spray does not. Bottom line: vegetable spray will keep the soufflés from sticking. But it's a definite flavor trade-off.

Frankly, I'd rather spend the 2 minutes it takes to butter the molds with my fingers.

Making the "hat"

Soufflés rise best if the upper edge of the batter is detached from the sides. After filling the prepared molds to the rim, level them with a narrow metal spatula. Grasp the edge of a mold with your thumb extending into the soufflé batter about 1/4 inch. Rotate the mold rapidly all the way around to create a "hat." Sometimes the soufflé batter is soft and you won't see a distinct "hat" forming. Nevertheless, you'll see the effect in the oven.

When is the Soufflé Done?

Adjust the oven rack to the specified position and preheat the oven to the directed temperature. *For individual soufflés,* set the ramekins well apart on a baking sheet and place in the oven. Most individual dessert soufflés bake in 10 minutes in a 400-degree F oven, during which time the soufflés will rise 1 inch or more above the rims. To test for doneness, insert a wooden skewer into the center of a soufflé right to the bottom. It should come out clean but the tip might appear moist. Aim for the soufflé to be cooked evenly throughout. If in doubt, underbake rather than overbake. It's better to have a soufflé with a slightly underdone center than one that is dry all the way through.

Roulades—soufflés baked in jelly-roll pans— are thin and bake in a few minutes. Test by pressing gently on the top; it should spring back when you release your finger. Soufflés baked *in a pie plate or on a platter* bake rather quickly, too.

Large soufflés tend to cook faster around the outsides than in their centers. To make the cooking more even, bake them at a lower temperature than individual soufflés. Choose a soufflé dish large enough to accommodate the risen soufflé without having to attach a paper or foil collar. The soufflé batter within the collar cooks at a different rate than in the soufflé mold. The best solution is to use a tall mold for the soufflé. Four-inch-tall charlotte molds made of tin work very well for both large savory and dessert soufflés. Test for doneness with a wooden skewer.

Gracious Serving

Hot soufflés should be served as soon as they come out of the oven, so have your guests seated and prepared for the drama. Soufflés retain their puff for a few minutes, but you want the maximum "wow" effect. If serving a *large soufflé,* once at the table, hold two large serving spoons vertically with their rounded sides touching each other just at the soufflé's surface. Insert one spoon an inch or so into the soufflé, following quickly with a similar action of the second spoon. Use the spoons to gently pull apart the soufflé and spoon portions onto plates. Pass any sauce separately.

For individual soufflés, set each onto a small serving plate before taking to the table. Use dinner teaspoons to eat, and be careful! The interiors of soufflés, especially dessert soufflés, are very hot.

Many hot dessert soufflé recipes say to dust the tops of the soufflés with confectioners' sugar before serving. While this makes for a very pretty presentation, it's easy to gag on the fine particles of sugar as you take in a breath while eating. So I just don't do it. Sometimes I'll sprinkle superfine sugar very lightly onto a soufflé's top either before (ramekins) or during (large mold) baking, for a delightful sugary crustiness.

Making Soufflés Ahead

Many soufflé batters may stand for an hour or so before baking and still puff as though they had been baked immediately. If the soufflé is in a large mold, just cover it with an upturned bowl and leave it undisturbed for the hour. Make sure the oven is preheated.

For longer storage, you can freeze an unbaked soufflé. I learned this from Madeleine Kamman in her groundbreaking book *The New Making of a Cook* (Morrow, 1997, page 177). Freeze the soufflés in individual ceramic molds by putting them on a tray in the coldest part of the freezer until they're frozen solid. Wrap each one in plastic wrap and then in foil, and store for up to a week. When you want to bake, take out the number you need, unwrap them, and let them sit at room temperature about 30 minutes. Preheat the oven while the soufflés partially thaw. Put the soufflés on a baking sheet and bake for about twice their normal baking time. Be sure to test for doneness with a wooden skewer.

CHAPTER 1

SOUFFLÉS DE CUISINE
Savory Soufflés

Soufflés are incredibly adaptable and accommodating. They can be easy or elegant; traditional or modern; sweet or savory; light as a feather or filled with flavorful surprises. They can be appetizers, main courses, side dishes and, of course, dessert.

In this chapter I explore the many different tastes and shapes of savory soufflés, from a simple, classic cheese soufflé, to a complex vegetable-filled soufflé roulade, to a fish soufflé baked on a platter and everything in between.

Vegetables such as cauliflower, fennel, corn, spinach, mushrooms, leeks, bell peppers, zucchini and broccoli have their time to shine, as do salmon, scallops and crab. And, as expected, luscious cheeses always play a part.

Savory soufflés can begin a meal, accompany a meal or be the star of the meal. So why not give one—or more—a try? Once you've become comfortable with soufflé making, experiment with your own flavor combinations.

SOUFFLÉ CLASSIQUE AU FROMAGE
Classic Cheese Soufflé

SERVES 4

Tall and majestic, with a crusty exterior and a super creamy interior, this quintessential French cheese soufflé is made the classic way, with a thick egg yolk-enriched béchamel lightened with stiffly beaten egg whites and flavored with shredded cheese. Folding the cheese into the béchamel along with the beaten whites, instead of stirring it in by itself, assures the ideal texture.

4 tablespoons unsalted butter, plus more for mold

2 tablespoons finely grated Parmesan cheese, for mold

1 cup whole milk, plus 1 tablespoon, divided

4 tablespoons all-purpose flour

1/2 teaspoon salt

1/4 teaspoon freshly ground black pepper

Pinch of freshly grated nutmeg

6 large eggs, separated, room temperature

Pinch of salt

1/4 teaspoon cream of tartar

1 cup (4 ounces) shredded Gruyère, Comté or P'tit Basque cheese

Adjust an oven rack to the lower third position and set a baking sheet on the rack. Preheat the oven to 400 degrees F. Butter bottom and sides of a 1 1/2-quart, 4-inch tall charlotte mold and coat with the Parmesan.

Heat 1 cup milk in a small heavy saucepan until bubbling but not boiling; keep warm. Melt 4 tablespoons butter in a medium heavy saucepan over medium heat. Stir in the flour with a wooden spoon and cook, stirring, for 2 minutes. Remove pan from the heat and whisk in the hot milk; sauce should be smooth. Return pan to medium-high heat and bring to the boil, whisking constantly. Cook and whisk until very thick, about 2 minutes. Remove pan from heat and whisk in the salt, pepper, and nutmeg. Whisk in the egg yolks one at a time. Film the surface of the béchamel with 1 tablespoon milk.

In the bowl of a stand mixer, beat the egg whites with a pinch of salt on medium speed until frothy, about 1 minute. Add cream of tartar and beat until soft peaks form. Increase speed to medium-high and continue beating until moist stiff peaks form, 1 to 2 minutes.

Stir about one-fourth of the whites into the béchamel to lighten. Gently fold in remaining whites, sprinkling in the shredded cheese as you fold. Fold until no white streaks remain. Transfer the batter into prepared mold, filling it about 3/4 inch from the top. (May be made to this point about 1 hour ahead. Cover mold with a large, upturned bowl.) Set the soufflé onto the baking sheet in the oven and bake until well browned on top, puffed about 2 inches above the rim, and a wooden skewer inserted into the center comes out clean but moist, about 25 minutes. Serve immediately.

SOUFFLÉS À L'AIL VERT
Green Garlic Soufflés

SERVES 6

Green garlic, or young garlic, is available in the spring and early summer. It resembles scallions but tastes mildly of garlic and lends a seductive flavor to soufflés and soups. This is a lovely appetizer for an elegant meal.

5 tablespoons unsalted butter, plus more for ramekins

2 tablespoons finely grated Parmesan cheese, plus more for ramekins

6 young green garlic plants, white to pale green part only (4 ounces), sliced thin to yield 1¼ cups

¾ cup water

¼ teaspoon salt

Freshly ground black pepper

1 cup whole milk, plus 1 tablespoon, divided

3 tablespoons all-purpose flour

½ teaspoon chopped fresh thyme

4 large eggs, separated, room temperature

Pinch of salt

¼ teaspoon cream of tartar

¾ cup shredded Gruyère cheese

Adjust an oven rack to the lower third position and preheat the oven to 400 degrees F. Butter bottom and sides of six 4- to 5-ounce ramekins, including the rims; coat with Parmesan cheese.

Melt 1 tablespoon butter in a medium heavy saucepan over medium heat. Add the green garlic, water and salt. Season with freshly ground pepper. Bring to a simmer, cover, and cook for 10 minutes. Uncover pan, increase heat to medium-high, and cook, stirring occasionally, until all the water has evaporated, 4 to 5 minutes. Reduce heat to medium-low. Add 1 cup milk and heat it to just below a simmer. Pour into a blender and purée until smooth.

Wash and dry the saucepan. Melt remaining 4 tablespoons butter in the pan over medium heat. Stir in the flour and thyme with a wooden spoon. Cook and stir 2 minutes. Remove pan from the heat. Whisk in the garlic purée and return pan to medium heat. Continue cooking, whisking constantly, until the sauce comes to the boil and has thickened slightly. Boil 1 minute, whisking constantly. Remove pan from heat and whisk in egg yolks one at a time. Film the top of the béchamel with 1 tablespoon milk to prevent a skin from forming. Sauce can be tepid to warm when folding in the beaten whites and cheese.

In the bowl of a stand mixer, beat the egg whites with salt on medium speed until frothy, about 1 minute. Add cream of tartar and beat until soft peaks form. Increase speed to medium-high and beat until moist stiff peaks form, 1 to 2 minutes.

Whisk the béchamel to smooth it out. Stir in one-fourth of the whites to lighten. Gently fold in the Gruyère alternately with remaining whites in three additions. Spoon the soufflé batter into prepared ramekins, filling almost to the top. Form a "hat" in each soufflé by running a thumb around the inside edge of the ramekin to disengage batter from the sides. Sprinkle tops of soufflés with the 2 tablespoons Parmesan. (May be made to this point about 1 hour ahead and covered loosely with plastic wrap. When ready to bake, space the uncovered ramekins well apart on a baking sheet.) Bake until soufflés are browned on top, the centers are slightly jiggly and a wooden skewer inserted into the center comes out clean but moist, 10 to 12 minutes. Serve immediately.

SOUFFLÉS AU SAUMON FUMÉ
Smoked Salmon Soufflés

SERVES 6

Here's a recipe for a simple yet sophisticated appetizer or first course. Use a good-quality smoked salmon that can be flaked, preferably wild-caught—not lox. This kind of salmon is packaged and refrigerated in chunks with skin attached.

2 tablespoons unsalted butter, plus more for ramekins

1/2 cup whole milk

1/2 cup half-and-half

3 tablespoons all-purpose flour

1/2 teaspoon salt

1/4 teaspoon freshly ground black pepper

Freshly grated nutmeg

2 large egg yolks

5 large egg whites (scant 2/3 cup), room temperature

Pinch of salt

1/4 teaspoon cream of tartar

8 ounces skinless and boneless smoked salmon, flaked with a fork

2 ounces (1/2 cup loosely packed) coarsely grated Gruyère or Comté cheese

3/4 cup crème fraîche

Adjust an oven rack to the center position and preheat oven to 425 degrees F. Butter bottom and sides of six 6-ounce ramekins.

Heat the milk and half-and-half in a small heavy saucepan until bubbling but not boiling; keep warm. Melt 2 tablespoons butter in a medium heavy saucepan over medium heat. Stir in the flour with a wooden spoon. Cook and stir 2 minutes. Remove pan from heat and whisk in the hot liquid; sauce should be smooth. Return pan to medium-high heat and bring to the boil, whisking constantly. Cook and whisk until very thick, about 2 minutes. Take pan off heat and whisk in the salt, pepper and nutmeg. Whisk in the egg yolks one at a time.

In the bowl of stand mixer, beat the egg whites with the salt on medium speed until frothy, about 1 minute. Add cream of tartar and beat until soft peaks form. Increase speed to medium-high and beat until moist stiff peaks form, 1 to 2 minutes. Fold whites into the béchamel, and then fold in the salmon and all but 2 tablespoons of the cheese.

Divide batter among ramekins, smooth tops with a metal spatula, and sprinkle with remaining cheese. Form a "hat" in each soufflé (see page 22). (May be made to this point about 1 hour ahead and covered loosely with plastic wrap.) When ready to bake, space uncovered ramekins well apart on a baking sheet. Bake until soufflés are nicely browned and puffed and a wooden skewer inserted in center comes out clean but moist, 10 to 12 minutes. Serve immediately on small plates and let each diner spoon crème fraîche into the center.

SOUFFLÉ AU CHOU-FLEUR
Cauliflower Soufflé

SERVES 6

Roasting cauliflower completely transforms the oft-maligned vegetable into something everyone can love, especially in this cheese-filled soufflé. My roasting technique, inspired from one created by Michael Ruhlman, brings optimum flavor to this béchamel-based soufflé. It is perfect as a side dish to roasted meats, fish or chicken. Serve with Sauce au Tomate.

8 tablespoons unsalted butter, room temperature, divided, plus more for baking dish

$1/4$ cup (1 ounce) finely grated Asiago cheese

1 head cauliflower, about $1^1/2$ pounds, trimmed

2 tablespoons olive oil

$1/2$ teaspoon salt

$1^1/4$ cups whole milk

$4^1/2$ tablespoons all-purpose flour

4 large egg yolks

$1/8$ teaspoon freshly grated nutmeg

Large pinch cayenne pepper

$1/2$ teaspoon salt

$1/4$ teaspoon freshly ground black pepper

6 large egg whites, room temperature

Pinch of salt

$1/4$ teaspoon cream of tartar

1 cup (4 ounces), grated Gruyère or Comté cheese

Sauce au Tomate (page 121)

Adjust an oven rack to the lower third position and preheat oven to 425 degrees F. Butter bottom and sides of a 2-quart baking dish. (For single servings, see page 33.) Coat with the Asiago cheese.

Place cauliflower into a 10-inch ovenproof skillet and rub olive oil all over it. Roast for 45 minutes. Remove from oven and rub 4 tablespoons butter all over the cauliflower. Sprinkle with $1/2$ teaspoon salt and bake until cauliflower is nicely browned and completely tender, 20 to 30 minutes more. Let cool until comfortable to touch. Cut the cauliflower into chunks and coarsely chop them. You will need 12 ounces ($2^1/2$ to 3 cups). (Can be prepared 1 day ahead; wrap and refrigerate.)

For the soufflé, with an oven rack still in the lower third position, preheat the oven to 425 degrees F. Heat milk in a small heavy saucepan until bubbling but not boiling; keep warm. Melt remaining 4 tablespoons butter in a medium heavy saucepan over medium heat. Stir in the flour with a wooden spoon. Cook and stir 2 minutes. Remove pan from heat and whisk in the hot milk; sauce should be smooth. Return pan to medium-high heat and bring to the boil, whisking constantly. Cook and whisk until very thick, about 2 minutes. Remove from heat and whisk in egg yolks one at a time. Whisk in the nutmeg, cayenne, salt and pepper. Fold in the chopped

continued >

cauliflower. Transfer the béchamel to a large bowl. Sauce can be tepid to warm when folding in the beaten whites and cheese.

In the bowl of a stand mixer, beat the egg whites with the salt on medium speed until frothy, about 1 minute. Add cream of tartar and beat until soft peaks form. Increase speed to medium-high and beat until moist stiff peaks form, 1 to 2 minutes. Stir one-fourth of the whites into the béchamel to lighten. Gently fold in remaining whites in two additions along with three-fourths of the grated Comté. Spread soufflé batter in prepared dish. Sprinkle top with remaining cheese. (May be made to this point about 1 hour ahead. Cover with an upturned pot.) Set the pan in the oven and reduce the heat to 400 degrees F.* Bake until the soufflé is puffed and browned and a wooden skewer inserted into the center comes out clean but moist, 25 to 30 minutes. Serve immediately with the Sauce au Tomate.

For single servings, as a vegetable course, butter and coat six 10-ounce molds (4 x 2$\frac{1}{2}$ inches) with finely grated Asiago. Fill ramekins to within $\frac{1}{2}$ inch of top. Form a "hat" in each soufflé by running a thumb around the inside edge of ramekin to disengage batter from the sides. (May be made to this point about 1 hour ahead and covered loosely with plastic wrap.) When ready to bake, space uncovered ramekins well apart on a baking sheet. Set pan in oven and reduce temperature to 400 degrees F. Bake about 25 minutes, until tops are browned, soufflés are well puffed and a wooden skewer inserted into the center comes out clean but moist. Serve immediately with Sauce au Tomate.

* Preheating oven at 425 degrees will give the soufflés a good heat boost to make the top nice and brown.

Soufflés au Fenouil
Fennel Soufflés

SERVES 4 AS A MAIN COURSE OR SIDE DISH, OR 8 AS AN APPETIZER

In the June 1978 issue of Cooking *magazine (a Cuisinart® publication), the editors published a translation of a French article on soufflés that had appeared in the March 1978 issue of Henri Gault and Christian Millau's monthly magazine,* Guide Gault-Millau de la France. *The two French journalists championed* la nouvelle cuisine *and the young chefs who created it. These chefs shunned flour-enriched béchamel bases for soufflés and replaced them with vegetable or fruit purées, capturing the pure flavor of the main ingredient. One recipe in the collection that caught my eye was for a soufflé that highlighted the faint anise flavor of fennel. At first I couldn't believe that the relatively thin base of cooked fennel would have enough body to sustain the soufflé's structure, but it did so beautifully, and it does so again here.*

2 tablespoons unsalted butter, plus more for ramekins

4 tablespoons fine dry unseasoned breadcrumbs, for ramekins

2 large fennel bulbs

2 tablespoons crème fraîche or heavy cream

4 large eggs, separated, plus 4 large egg whites, room temperature

³/₄ teaspoon salt

¹/₄ teaspoon freshly ground pepper

Freshly grated nutmeg

Pinch of salt

¹/₂ teaspoon cream of tartar

Adjust an oven rack to the lower third position and preheat the oven to 400 degrees F. Butter bottom and sides of four 1^1/$_2$-cup (12-ounce) ramekins (for main course or side dish) or eight 4- to 5-ounce ramekins (for side dish). Coat the ramekins with breadcrumbs, shaking out excess.

Cut the feathery stalks off the fennel bulbs and reserve for another use if desired. Trim off root ends and remove blemished outside layers. You will need 8 ounces of trimmed bulbs. Cut the bulbs into 1-inch chunks. Place chunks in a food processor and pulse until finely chopped. The fennel will start to darken within a few minutes, but that is fine. Put fennel into a medium heavy saucepan and add the crème fraîche and the 2 tablespoons butter. Cook over medium heat for 2 to 3 minutes, stirring often. Reduce heat to medium-low, cover pan and cook until the fennel is tender, about 10 minutes more, stirring occasionally. Transfer cooked fennel back to the food processor and pulse a few times to chop a bit more. (Can be prepared up to 1 day ahead; cool, cover and refrigerate. Rewarm gently before continuing.) Add the egg yolks and process 5 seconds to combine. Scrape down sides of the work bowl. Add the salt, pepper and a few pinches or gratings of nutmeg and pulse twice. Transfer fennel to a large bowl. Fennel can be tepid to warm when folding in the beaten whites.

In the bowl of a stand mixer, beat the 8 egg whites with a pinch of salt on medium speed until frothy, about 1 minute. Add cream of tartar and beat until soft peaks form. Increase speed to medium-high and beat until moist stiff peaks form, 1 to 2 minutes.

Stir about one-fifth of the whites into the fennel. Gently fold in remaining whites until no white streaks remain. Divide soufflé batter among prepared ramekins, filling right to the tops or even slightly above. Form a "hat" in each soufflé by running a thumb around the inside edge of the ramekin to disengage batter from the sides. Space ramekins well apart on a large baking sheet. These soufflés are best when baked right away. Bake until puffed at least an inch above the rims, the tops are nicely browned with a few cracks and a wooden skewer inserted into the center comes out clean but moist, 10 to 12 minutes for the larger ramekins and 8 minutes for the smaller ramekins. Serve immediately.

Soufflé au Maïs Frais
Fresh Corn Soufflé

SERVES 6

This is one of the best soufflés I know. It has a sublime flavor, and the texture of the creamy interior makes for a wonderful contrast with the al dente corn kernels and peppers as well as the crunchy and cheesy sides and bottom.

8 tablespoons unsalted butter, divided, plus more for baking dish

6 ounces ($^3/_4$ cup) finely grated Gruyère or Comté cheese

3 garlic cloves, minced

2 cups fresh corn kernels cut off the cob (about 4 ears) or frozen corn kernels, thawed

$^1/_2$ cup diced ($^1/_4$-inch) red bell pepper

2 teaspoons seeded and finely chopped jalapeño pepper

$^3/_4$ teaspoon salt, divided

$^1/_2$ teaspoon freshly ground black pepper, divided

$^3/_4$ cup whole milk

$^3/_4$ cup half-and-half

5 tablespoons all-purpose flour

6 large eggs, separated, room temperature

Pinch of salt

$^1/_4$ teaspoon cream of tartar

Adjust an oven rack to the lower third position and preheat oven to 400 degrees F. Butter bottom and sides of a 2$^1/_2$-quart (10 x 2-inch) round or oval baking dish and coat with 2 ounces ($^1/_4$ cup) of the cheese. It will not cover the inside of the baking dish completely; there will be gaps.

Melt 4 tablespoons butter in a medium heavy skillet over medium heat. Add the garlic and stir about 15 seconds. Add the corn, red bell pepper and jalapeño and cook, stirring occasionally, until the pepper and corn are partly tender, 2 to 3 minutes. Season with $^1/_4$ teaspoon salt and $^1/_4$ teaspoon pepper.

Heat the milk and half-and-half in a small heavy saucepan over medium heat until bubbling but not boiling; keep warm. Melt the remaining 4 tablespoons butter in a medium heavy saucepan over medium heat. Stir in the flour with a wooden spoon. Cook and stir for 2 minutes. Remove pan from heat and whisk in the hot liquid; sauce should be smooth. Return pan to medium-high heat and bring to the boil, whisking constantly. Cook and whisk until very thick, about 2 minutes. Remove from heat and whisk in egg yolks one at a time. Season béchamel with $^1/_2$ teaspoon salt and $^1/_4$ teaspoon pepper and transfer to a large bowl. Sauce can be tepid to warm when folding in the beaten whites and cheese.

In the bowl of a stand mixer, beat the egg whites with a pinch of salt on medium speed until frothy, about 1 minute. Add cream of tartar and beat until soft peaks form. Increase speed to medium-high and beat until moist stiff peaks form, 1 to 2 minutes. Whisk one-fourth of the whites into the béchamel. Gently fold in remaining whites in two additions, then fold in the cooled corn, red pepper and jalapeño and the remaining 4 ounces (1 cup) of cheese. Spread the soufflé batter in the prepared dish. (May be made to this point about 1 hour ahead. Cover with a large upturned pot.) Bake until quite puffy, well browned and a wooden skewer inserted into the center comes out clean but moist, about 30 minutes. Serve immediately.

SOUFFLÉ AUX EPINARDS ET CHAMPIGNONS
Spinach and Mushroom Soufflé

SERVES 6

Spinach and mushrooms are a match made in heaven, whether in an omelette or in this fabulous soufflé. Because both vegetables contain a great deal of water, they receive a preliminary cooking to remove the water and concentrate their flavors. This soufflé is perfect for brunch, lunch or supper, accompanied by a crusty bread and a crisp chilled white wine such as Vouvray.

3^1/$_2$ tablespoons unsalted butter, divided, plus more for mold

2 tablespoons finely grated Parmesan cheese, for mold

1 pound fresh spinach, washed and stemmed

1 tablespoon olive oil

2 tablespoons minced shallot

4 ounces mushrooms, minced

^{1}/$_8$ teaspoon freshly grated nutmeg

^{3}/$_4$ teaspoon salt, divided

^{1}/$_2$ teaspoon freshly ground pepper, divided

1 cup whole milk

3 tablespoons all-purpose flour

4 large egg yolks

5 large egg whites (scant ^{2}/$_3$ cup), room temperature

Pinch of salt

^{1}/$_4$ teaspoon cream of tartar

2 ounces (^{1}/$_2$ cup) grated cheese such as Gruyère, Comté, or P'tit Basque

Adjust an oven rack to the lower third position and preheat oven to 400 degrees F. Butter bottom and sides of a 6-cup soufflé or charlotte mold and coat with the Parmesan cheese.

Bring a large pot of water to the boil. Add the spinach, return water to the boil and cook, uncovered, for 2 minutes. Drain in a colander and rinse under cold water until spinach is cool. Squeeze handfuls of spinach to remove as much water as possible. You should have about ^{1}/$_2$ cup spinach. Chop the spinach.

Melt 1 tablespoon butter with the oil in a 10-inch heavy skillet over medium-high heat. Add the shallot. Stir and cook for a few seconds. Add the minced mushrooms and stir and cook until the mushroom pieces begin to separate from one another, 2 to 3 minutes. Add the chopped spinach and cook, stirring, 2 to 3 minutes more. Stir in the nutmeg, ^{1}/$_4$ teaspoon salt and ^{1}/$_4$ teaspoon pepper. You should have about ^{3}/$_4$ cup of spinach and mushrooms. (May be made 4 to 5 hours ahead; cover and refrigerate.)

Heat milk in small heavy saucepan over medium heat until bubbling but not boiling; keep warm. Melt the remaining 2 1/2 tablespoons butter in a medium heavy saucepan over medium heat. Stir in the flour with a wooden spoon. Cook and stir 2 minutes. Remove pan from heat and whisk in hot milk; sauce should be smooth. Return pan to medium-high heat and bring to the boil, whisking constantly. Cook and whisk until very thick, about 2 minutes. Remove pan from heat and whisk in the egg yolks one at a time. Stir in remaining 1/2 teaspoon salt and 1/4 teaspoon pepper. Stir in spinach and mushrooms. Sauce can be tepid to warm when folding in the beaten whites and cheese.

In the bowl of a stand mixer, beat the egg whites with a pinch of salt on medium speed until frothy, about 1 minute. Add cream of tartar and beat until soft peaks form. Increase speed to medium-high and beat until moist stiff peaks form, 1 to 2 minutes. Stir one-fourth of the whites into the spinach and mushroom béchamel to lighten. Gently fold in remaining whites and the cheese in two additions, folding just until no white streaks remain. Transfer the soufflé batter into prepared mold. (May be made about 1 hour ahead. Cover with an upturned pot.) Place the uncovered mold in the oven and lower oven heat to 375 degrees F. Bake until the soufflé is puffed, the top is lightly browned, and a skewer inserted into the center comes out clean but moist, about 30 minutes. Serve immediately.

Soufflé au Crabe et aux Morilles

Crab and Morel Mushroom Soufflé

SERVES 4

This luxurious soufflé, which brings together two spectacular ingredients, is ideal for a special-occasion brunch, lunch or dinner. Serve it as a main course accompanied by a simple salad and sparkling wine; follow with a fruit dessert. Fresh morel mushrooms are available in the spring, so substitute dried reconstituted morels when fresh aren't in season.

6 tablespoons unsalted butter, plus more for dish

$1/4$ cup unseasoned fine dry breadcrumbs

$1/2$ cup finely chopped sweet onion such as Walla Walla or Vidalia

1 cup (3 ounces) diced fresh morel mushrooms or 1 ounce rehydrated dried morel mushrooms, drained and diced

8 ounces fresh lump crabmeat, picked over

$1^1/2$ tablespoons finely chopped fresh tarragon

1 tablespoon dry sherry

$3/4$ teaspoon salt, divided

$1/2$ teaspoon freshly ground black pepper, divided

1 cup half-and-half

$1/2$ cup fish stock or bottled clam juice

$4^1/2$ tablespoons all-purpose flour

$1/8$ teaspoon freshly grated nutmeg

4 large egg yolks

Freshly squeezed lemon juice

5 large egg whites, room temperature

Pinch of salt

$1/4$ teaspoon cream of tartar

$1/4$ cup (1 ounce) shredded Gruyère or Comté cheese

Adjust an oven rack to the center position, set a baking sheet on the rack, and preheat oven to 425 degrees F. Butter bottom and sides of a 2-quart baking dish and dust the inside with breadcrumbs, shaking out the excess.

Melt 2 tablespoons butter in a 10-inch heavy skillet over medium heat. Add onion and cook, stirring occasionally, until translucent, 6 to 8 minutes. (If you are concerned onion will cook too fast and brown, then lower heat to medium-low and cook for 10 minutes, or cover and sweat.) Add the morels and cook, stirring, until mushrooms are tender, a few minutes more. Using a flexible spatula, fold in the crabmeat, tarragon, and sherry. Be gentle so as not to break apart the pieces of crab. Season with $1/4$ teaspoon salt and $1/4$ teaspoon pepper. Keep warm over lowest heat.

Heat the half-and-half and fish stock or clam juice in a small heavy saucepan until bubbling but not boiling; keep warm. Melt the remaining 4 tablespoons butter in a medium heavy saucepan over medium heat. Stir in the flour with a wooden spoon. Cook and stir for 2 minutes. Remove pan from heat and whisk in hot liquid; sauce should be smooth. Return pan to medium-high heat and bring to the boil, whisking constantly. Cook and whisk until very thick, about 2 minutes. Whisk in remaining ½ teaspoon salt, ¼ teaspoon pepper, and the nutmeg. Whisk in egg yolks one at a time. Taste and adjust seasoning with additional salt and pepper. Add droplets of lemon juice to taste. Fold in the crab and mushrooms. Sauce can be tepid to warm when folding in the beaten whites.

In the bowl of a stand mixture, beat the egg whites with a pinch of salt on medium speed until frothy, about 1 minute. Add cream of tartar and beat until soft peaks form. Increase speed to medium-high and beat until moist stiff peaks form, 1 to 2 minutes. Gently fold one-fourth of the whites into the crab and mushroom béchamel to lighten. Fold in remaining whites until no white streaks remain. Transfer the soufflé batter into prepared dish. Smooth the top and sprinkle with the shredded cheese. (May be made about 1 hour ahead and covered with an upturned pot.) Place uncovered dish in the oven on the baking sheet. Immediately reduce oven temperature to 375 degrees F.* Bake 25 to 30 minutes, until the soufflé is puffed and well browned on top and a wooden skewer inserted into the center come out clean but moist. Do not underbake; the center of the soufflé is always the last to rise. Serve immediately.

*Preheating oven at higher temperature will give a heat boost and make sure the top is a really nice brown.

SOUFFLÉS AU ROQUEFORT
Roquefort Soufflés

SERVES 8

These intensely flavored soufflés make an excellent appetizer. Make sure to use genuine Roquefort cheese for its unique taste.

2^1/$_2$ tablespoons unsalted butter, plus more for
    ramekins
2 ounces (^{1}/$_2$ cup) grated Parmesan cheese for
    ramekins
1 cup whole milk
3 tablespoons all-purpose flour
^{1}/$_4$ teaspoon hot pepper sauce

^{1}/$_8$ teaspoon salt
^{1}/$_4$ cup packed crumbled Roquefort cheese
4 large eggs, separated, room temperature
2 tablespoons finely chopped fresh Italian parsley
Pinch of salt
^{1}/$_4$ teaspoon cream of tartar

Adjust an oven rack to the lower third position and preheat oven to 400 degrees F. Butter bottom and sides of eight 4- to 5-ounce ramekins and coat each with 1 tablespoon of the Parmesan cheese.

Heat milk in a small heavy saucepan until bubbling but not boiling; keep warm. Melt 2^1/$_2$ tablespoons butter in a medium saucepan over medium heat. Stir in the flour with a wooden spoon. Cook and stir 2 minutes. Remove pan from heat and whisk in the milk; sauce should be smooth. Whisk in the hot pepper sauce and salt. Return pan to medium-high heat and bring to the boil, whisking constantly. Cook and whisk until very thick, about 2 minutes. Remove pan from heat and whisk in the Roquefort cheese until melted and smooth. Whisk in the egg yolks one at a time, then the parsley. Transfer the béchamel to a large bowl. Sauce can be tepid to warm when folding in the beaten whites.

In the bowl of a stand mixer, beat the egg whites and a pinch of salt on medium speed until frothy, about 1 minute. Add cream of tartar and beat until soft peaks form. Increase speed to medium-high and beat until moist stiff peaks form, 1 to 2 minutes. Add the whites to the Roquefort béchamel and gently fold until no white streaks remain.

Divide the soufflé batter among prepared ramekins, filling them about ^{1}/$_2$ inch from the tops. Form a "hat" in each soufflé by running a thumb around the inside edge of ramekin to disengage batter from the sides. (May be made to this point about 1 hour ahead and covered loosely with plastic wrap.) When ready to bake, space uncovered ramekins well apart on a baking sheet. Bake until puffed and golden brown on top and a wooden skewer inserted into the center comes out clean but moist, 10 to 12 minutes. Serve immediately.

SOUFFLÉ SENS DESSUS DESSOUS AUX POIREAUX ET À LA PANCETTA

Topsy-Turvy Leek and Pancetta Soufflé

SERVES 6

For a marvelous appetizer, here's a soufflé that you bake and then upend onto a serving platter, cut into portions, and serve with Sauce au Tomate (page 121). Leeks, pancetta and Gruyère or Comté cheese flavor the soufflé, and Dijon mustard and cayenne pepper supply a welcome bite. The soufflé bakes slowly in a water bath for over an hour to give it an even, creamy texture throughout.

2 tablespoons unsalted butter, plus more for mold

3 tablespoons fine dry unseasoned breadcrumbs, for mold

1 tablespoon olive oil

2 ounces pancetta, finely chopped

6 ounces ($1^{1}/_{2}$ cups) thinly sliced white and pale green part of leeks, about 2 leeks, washed well to remove any grit

2 tablespoons dry white French vermouth

$^{3}/_{4}$ teaspoons salt, divided

$^{1}/_{2}$ teaspoon freshly ground pepper, divided

$^{3}/_{4}$ cup whole milk

3 tablespoons all-purpose flour

$1^{1}/_{2}$ teaspoons Dijon mustard

$^{1}/_{4}$ teaspoon cayenne pepper

3 large egg yolks

6 large egg whites ($^{3}/_{4}$ cup), room temperature

Pinch of salt

$^{1}/_{4}$ teaspoon cream of tartar

4 ounces (1 cup loosely packed) coarsely grated Gruyère or Comté cheese

Sauce au Tomate (page 121)

Parsley sprigs

Set an empty 8-cup charlotte mold or baking dish into a 3-inch-deep roasting pan and, holding the mold in place so it doesn't float, add enough water to roasting pan to come halfway up the sides of the mold. Remove mold and dry it. Bring the water in the roasting pan to a simmer and keep water hot.

Adjust an oven rack to the lower third position and preheat the oven to 350 degrees F. Butter the bottom and sides of the mold. Coat with breadcrumbs, shaking out excess.

Heat the olive oil in a 10-inch heavy skillet over high heat. Add the pancetta and stir with a wooden spoon. Reduce heat to medium and cook until pancetta is browned and crisp, stirring often, about 2 minutes. Add the leeks and vermouth. Stir well, cover and reduce the heat to low.

continued >

Cook until leeks are tender, stirring occasionally, 10 to 15 minutes. Cool leeks to room temperature. Season with $\frac{1}{4}$ teaspoon salt and $\frac{1}{4}$ teaspoon pepper. (Can be prepared 1 hour ahead.)

Heat milk in a small heavy saucepan over medium heat until bubbling but not boiling; keep warm. Melt the 2 tablespoons butter in a medium heavy saucepan over medium heat. Stir in the flour with a wooden spoon. Cook and stir for 2 minutes. Remove pan from heat and whisk in the hot milk; sauce should be smooth. Return pan to medium-high heat and bring to the boil, whisking constantly. Cook and whisk until very thick, about 2 minutes. Remove pan from heat. Whisk in the mustard, remaining $\frac{1}{2}$ teaspoon salt, $\frac{1}{4}$ teaspoon black pepper, and cayenne. Whisk in the egg yolks one at a time. Transfer béchamel into a large bowl. Whisk occasionally to prevent a skin from forming. Sauce can be tepid to warm when folding in the beaten whites and cheese.

Set the roasting pan with hot water in the oven.

In the bowl of a stand mixer, beat the whites and a pinch of salt on medium speed until frothy, about 1 minute. Add cream of tartar and beat until soft peaks form. Increase speed to medium-high and beat until moist stiff peaks form, 1 to 2 minutes. Whisk one-fourth of the whites into the béchamel to lighten. Add half the remaining whites, half the leeks and pancetta and half the cheese. Fold together gently but thoroughly. Repeat with remaining whites, leeks and pancetta, and cheese. Transfer soufflé batter to prepared mold—it will fill the mold by about half—and put the mold into the roasting pan filled with hot water. Bake until the soufflé is well puffed and crusty on top and fills the soufflé dish and a wooden skewer inserted into the center comes out clean but moist, 60 to 75 minutes.

Heat the Sauce au Tomate. Remove soufflé from the water bath. Turn a warm serving platter over the soufflé; grasp the two together with pot holders and invert. Wait a few seconds and lift off the mold. The soufflé will be an even golden brown color. Spoon the hot Sauce au Tomate all around the soufflé and a little on top. Garnish with parsley sprigs and bring to the table. Cut into portions with a sharp knife and serve at once with extra sauce.

SOUFFLÉ AUX COQUILLES SAINT-JACQUES
Scallop Soufflé

SERVES 4 TO 6

Scallops, herbs and cheese marry deliciously in this impressive dish for a dinner party, whether as a first course for six people or as a main course for four. (If serving as a main course, accompany with a nice tossed green salad or a salad of cucumbers and tomatoes.) Either way, pour a chilled crisp dry white wine such as Sancerre or Chablis. Try to find fresh—never frozen—sea scallops, as frozen ones release too much liquid when thawed. Check each scallop to see if there's a narrow muscle attached on the side. If so, cut it away and discard.

5 tablespoons unsalted butter, divided, plus more for baking dish

1 tablespoon olive oil

2 tablespoons minced shallot

1 garlic clove, minced

1 1/4 pounds trimmed fresh sea scallops, patted dry, cut in half crosswise

3 tablespoons finely chopped fresh flat-leaf parsley

1 tablespoon finely chopped fresh tarragon

1 teaspoon salt, divided

Freshly ground black pepper

3/4 cup whole milk

3/4 cup half-and-half

4 tablespoons all-purpose flour

Pinch of cayenne pepper

Pinch of freshly grated nutmeg

4 large egg yolks

6 large egg whites (3/4 cup), room temperature

Pinch of salt

1/4 teaspoon cream of tartar

4 ounces (1 cup) coarsely shredded Comté or Gruyère cheese

1 1/2 ounces (about 1/3 cup) coarsely shredded P'tit Basque or more Comté or Gruyère.

Adjust an oven rack to the lower third position, set a baking sheet on the rack, and preheat oven to 350 degrees F. Butter bottom and sides of a 2 1/2-quart round or oval baking dish that is 2 inches deep.

Melt 2 tablespoons butter with the olive oil in a large heavy skillet over medium-high heat. Add the shallot and garlic and stir with a wooden spoon for a few seconds. Add the scallops. Sprinkle with parsley, tarragon and 1/2 teaspoon salt. Season with pepper and toss scallops around the pan for 1 minute; do not overcook. Transfer scallops and any liquid in the pan into prepared baking dish. As the scallops cool, juices will collect.

continued >

Heat the milk and half-and-half in small heavy saucepan over medium heat to bubbling but not boiling; keep warm. Melt remaining 3 tablespoons butter in a medium heavy saucepan over medium heat. Stir in the flour with a wooden spoon. Cook and stir 2 minutes. Remove pan from heat and whisk in the hot liquid; sauce should be smooth. Return pan to medium-high heat and bring to the boil, whisking constantly. Cook and whisk until very thick, about 2 minutes. Remove pan from heat and whisk in remaining $1/2$ teaspoon salt, cayenne and nutmeg. Whisk in the egg yolks one at a time. Adjust béchamel seasoning with additional salt and pepper. Transfer to a large bowl. Sauce can be tepid to warm when folding in the beaten whites and cheese.

In the bowl of stand mixer, beat the egg whites with a pinch of salt on medium speed until frothy, about 1 minute. Add cream of tartar and beat until soft peaks form. Increase speed to medium-high and beat until moist stiff peaks form, 1 to 2 minutes. Whisk one-fourth of the egg whites into the béchamel to lighten, but don't be too thorough. (White streaks are okay until the end of the process.) Gently fold half the remaining whites and half the Comté or Gruyère cheese into the béchamel. Again, don't be too thorough at this point. Gently fold remaining whites and cheese into béchamel just until no white streaks remain. Spread soufflé batter over the scallops. Sprinkle the P'tit Basque or Comté or Gruyère on top; dish will be very full. Put the soufflé on the baking sheet in the oven. Bake until the soufflé is well puffed, nicely browned and crusty on top, and a wooden skewer inserted into the center comes out clean but moist, 30 to 35 minutes. Divide soufflé among plates, spooning scallops and their juices alongside.

SOUFFLÉ AU SAUMON SUR LE PLAT AVEC UNE SAUCE MOUSSELINE À L'OSEILLE

Salmon Soufflé on a Platter with Sorrel Mousseline Sauce

SERVES 4

Many years ago I watched Julia Child prepare a fish soufflé on a platter on her black-and-white TV series, The French Chef. *During that half hour she went through all the steps of poaching the fish, making the soufflé and sauce, and baking and serving the final dish. Her closing words were, and I'm paraphrasing: "If you've mastered egg yolk cookery and whipping egg whites for a soufflé, then you're a real cook." At the time, as a newlywed, I hadn't mastered any branch of cookery, but her words motivated me and set me on my path as a cook. This recipe is my homage to Julia. It's classically French and tastes fantastic. Serve it with a lovely white wine and as you raise your glass say "bon appétit" as a toast to Julia Child.*

I like to serve this soufflé with a sorrel sauce. Sorrel is a perennial herb with deep roots that grows in the spring and summer. It has slender pointy leaves and a bright acidic flavor from its content of oxalic acid. In the amounts used in soups, stews, and sauces, sorrel is perfectly safe. There is no substitute. However, you may use spinach and lemon juice if you can't find sorrel.

Fish

1 cup fish stock plus $^{1}/_{2}$ cup dry white vermouth, or $^{1}/_{2}$ cup each of water, bottled clam juice, and dry white vermouth

1 pound skinless, boneless salmon or steelhead trout, cut into 4 pieces

3 tablespoons minced shallot

6 parsley sprigs

1 bay leaf

Salt and freshly ground black pepper

Soufflé Batter

$^{3}/_{4}$ cup milk

$^{1}/_{4}$ cup reduced fish-cooking liquid

3 tablespoons unsalted butter, plus more for platter

3 tablespoons all-purpose flour

2 large egg yolks

Salt and freshly ground black pepper

Pinch of freshly grated nutmeg

1 to 2 tablespoons heavy cream

5 large egg whites, room temperature

Pinch of salt

$^{1}/_{4}$ teaspoon cream of tartar

$^{1}/_{2}$ cup (2 ounces) shredded Gruyère or Comté cheese

Sorrel Mousseline Sauce

1 tablespoon unsalted butter

1 bunch sorrel,* tough stems removed, leaves cut into thin strips (about $1^{1}/_{2}$ cups loosely packed)

3 large egg yolks

$^{1}/_{3}$ cup heavy cream

$^{1}/_{4}$ cup reduced fish-cooking liquid

8 tablespoons unsalted butter, room temperature

Salt and freshly ground black pepper

3 tablespoons finely chopped fresh flat-leaf parsley

* *If sorrel is unavailable, use an equal amount of finely chopped washed spinach leaves and lemon juice to taste.*

continued >

For the fish, pour the liquid into a 3- to 4-quart nonreactive saucepan. Add the fish, shallot, parsley and bay leaf. Season lightly with salt and pepper. (Be careful with the salt if using clam juice since it is already salted.) The liquid should just barely cover the fish. Add a bit more water to cover if necessary. Set the pan over medium-low heat and bring the liquid to just below a simmer; do not boil. Cook the fish slowly until it is just cooked through or is slightly underdone, about 5 minutes, once the liquid is hot. Remove fish from the liquid and transfer to a plate. Strain the liquid, discarding solids. Return liquid to the pan and boil down to $1/2$ cup. Taste to see how salty it is. This will help you decide how much salt to add to the soufflé base and the Sorrel Mousseline Sauce. Transfer the liquid to a small bowl.

If not continuing with the recipe at this point, cover the fish and reduced liquid with plastic wrap and refrigerate for up to 8 hours. Bring to room temperature when ready to complete the dish.

Soufflé Batter

Adjust an oven rack to the upper middle position and preheat oven to 375 degrees F. Butter a large oval ovenproof serving platter measuring about 16 x 10 inches or a round one measuring about 12 inches in diameter. You can also use a 12-inch skillet or sauté pan.

Heat milk and $1/4$ cup fish-cooking liquid in small heavy saucepan until bubbling but not boiling; keep warm. Melt 3 tablespoons butter in a medium heavy saucepan over medium heat. Stir in the flour with a wooden spoon and cook, stirring, 2 minutes. Remove pan from heat and whisk in hot liquid; sauce should be smooth. Return pan to medium-high heat and bring to the boil, whisking constantly. Cook and whisk until very thick, about 2 minutes. Remove from heat and whisk in the egg yolks one at a time. Taste carefully and season béchamel with salt, pepper and nutmeg. Film the top with the heavy cream to prevent a skin from forming.

In the bowl of a stand mixer, beat the egg whites and a pinch of salt on medium speed until frothy, about 1 minute. Add cream of tartar and continue beating until soft peaks form. Increase speed to medium-high and beat until moist stiff peaks form, 1 to 2 minutes. Whisk one-fourth of the whites into béchamel to lighten. Gently fold in remaining whites and half the cheese until no white streaks remain.

Spread a thin layer of soufflé batter onto the prepared platter, using about one-fifth of the batter. Break the fish up into large flakes and place 4 mounds spaced a few inches apart atop the batter. Spoon remaining batter over the fish to cover completely and sprinkle remaining cheese onto the mounds. Bake until the soufflé is puffed and well browned, about 25 minutes.

While the soufflé bakes, make the sauce. Melt 1 tablespoon butter in a small heavy saucepan over medium heat. Using a wooden spoon, stir in the sorrel and continue cooking until it is wilted and has turned a drab green color, about 2 minutes. The sorrel will shrink to a couple of tablespoons. (If substituting spinach, per footnote, cook 3 to 4 minutes, until spinach is completely tender. Take pan off heat and stir in lemon juice $1/2$ teaspoon at a time until spinach has a bright acidic flavor.)

Put the egg yolks into a medium heavy saucepan. Whisk yolks vigorously until thick, about 1 minute. Whisk in the heavy cream and remaining ¼ cup reduced fish-cooking liquid. Set the pan over medium or medium-low heat and cook, stirring constantly with a heatproof rubber spatula, to make a custard sauce that just barely thickens, about 8 minutes. Watch carefully that the yolks don't curdle. Remove pan from heat periodically to check consistency of the sauce. You'll see wisps of steam rising just about the time the sauce has thickened properly. A thermometer will register between 175 and 180 degrees F.

Remove from heat and whisk in the 8 tablespoons butter 1 tablespoon at a time. The sauce will be light and have bubbles. Taste and adjust seasoning with salt and pepper. Stir in the cooked sorrel and parsley. Keep sauce warm by setting the pan into a skillet of tepid water.

As soon as the soufflé is done, cut between the mounds with a knife and loosen portions with a metal spatula. Set portions on heated plates and spoon generous amount of sauce over the soufflé. Serve immediately.

Soufflé "Roulade" aux Champignons, Courgettes et Poivrons

Soufflé Roulade with Mushrooms, Zucchini and Bell Peppers

SERVES 6

Here's another way to make a soufflé: bake it in a jelly-roll pan, fill it with sautéed savory vegetables, roll it up, slice it and serve with a creamy sauce. Quite ingenious, oh so delicious and perfect as a vegetarian main course. While I have used mushrooms, zucchini and bell peppers, other vegetables would work just as well. The sauce I serve with the roulade is a combination of a béchamel and velouté. Does that make it a béchouté or a vélamel?

Vegetables

³/₄ pound cremini mushrooms

2 tablespoons butter

4 tablespoons olive oil, divided

2 teaspoons salt, divided

³/₈ teaspoon freshly ground black pepper, divided

1 pound zucchini, about 3 medium

1 large onion (about 8 ounces), peeled, halved vertically and thinly sliced

2 garlic cloves, minced

3 large green, red, yellow and/or orange bell peppers (about 1¹/₂ pounds total), cored, seeded, and cut unto ¹/₄-inch-wide strips

4 tablespoons chopped fresh basil

2 teaspoons chopped fresh thyme

2 tablespoons chopped fresh parsley

Soufflé Batter

6 tablespoons unsalted butter, divided, plus more for pan

¹/₃ cup all-purpose flour, plus more for pan

¹/₃ cup panko breadcrumbs

1¹/₂ cups whole milk, plus 1 to 2 tablespoons, divided

6 large eggs, separated, room temperature

¹/₈ teaspoon freshly grated nutmeg

¹/₂ teaspoon salt

¹/₄ teaspoon freshly ground pepper

Pinch of salt

¹/₄ teaspoon cream of tartar

1 cup (4 ounces) coarsely grated Comté cheese

Serving Sauce

Reserved zucchini juice

Whole milk

¹/₃ cup heavy cream

4 tablespoons unsalted butter, divided

3 tablespoons unbleached all-purpose flour

Salt and freshly ground black pepper

Freshly grated nutmeg

For the vegetables, separate mushroom caps from the stems and cut both into ¼-inch dice. Melt the butter with 1 tablespoon olive oil in a large heavy skillet over medium-high heat. Add the mushrooms and toss to coat. Cook, tossing occasionally, until mushrooms take on a shine and are nicely browned and cooked through, 3 to 5 minutes. Cool and season with ¼ teaspoon salt and ⅛ teaspoon pepper.

Cut the ends off the zucchini. Set a box grater in a large bowl. Shred the zucchini on the large holes of the grater into the bowl. Toss zucchini with 1 teaspoon salt. Let stand 1 hour. Squeeze zucchini by handfuls over another bowl to extract as much liquid as possible. Cover liquid and refrigerate until ready to use. Set shredded zucchini aside.

Heat remaining 3 tablespoons olive oil in a large heavy skillet over medium heat. Stir in the onion, cover and cook without browning until translucent and almost tender, about 6 minutes, stirring occasionally. Stir in the garlic. Add the shredded zucchini and cook until almost tender, stirring and tossing constantly, about 5 minutes. Add the peppers and herbs. Season with remaining ¾ teaspoon salt and remaining ¼ teaspoon pepper. Toss and stir to combine. Reduce heat to low, cover and cook until the peppers are tender, stirring occasionally, about 20 minutes. Uncover the pan, and if there are any juices, raise the heat to medium-high and cook, stirring constantly, until the liquid has evaporated. Remove from heat and cool uncovered. (Can be prepared 1 to 2 days ahead; cover and refrigerate.) Reheat when ready to assemble the soufflé.

Adjust an oven rack to the center position and preheat oven to 425 degrees F. Butter a 15½ x 10½ x 1-inch jelly-roll pan. Line pan with parchment or wax paper, allowing for an overhang of about 2 inches at each end. Butter the paper and dust all over with flour, shaking out excess.

Combine the panko breadcrumbs and 2 tablespoons butter in a small heavy skillet over medium heat and toast, stirring frequently, until the crumbs are golden brown, about 5 minutes.

For the soufflé batter, heat 1½ cups milk in a small heavy saucepan until bubbling but not boiling; keep warm. Melt remaining 4 tablespoons butter in a medium heavy saucepan over medium heat. Stir in the flour with a wooden spoon. Cook and stir 2 minutes. Remove pan from heat and whisk in hot milk; sauce should be smooth. Return pan to medium-high heat and bring to the boil, whisking constantly. Cook and whisk until very thick, about 2 minutes. Remove pan from heat and whisk in the egg yolks one at a time. Whisk in nutmeg, salt and pepper. Scrape into a large bowl and film the top of the béchamel with 1 to 2 tablespoons cold milk to prevent a skin from forming. Sauce can be tepid to warm when folding in the beaten whites and cheese.

In the bowl of a stand mixer, beat the egg whites with a pinch of salt on medium speed until frothy, about 1 minute. Add cream of tartar and beat until soft peaks form. Increase speed to medium-high, and beat until moist stiff peaks form, 1 to 2 minutes.

Whisk the béchamel until smooth. Whisk in one-fourth of the whites to lighten. Gently fold in remaining whites. Sprinkle on the cheese as you fold, and fold just until no white streaks

continued >

remain. Spread the soufflé batter evenly and gently in prepared pan. Bake about 10 minutes, until soufflé has puffed, springs back when gently pressed in the center, and is nicely browned on top with large cracks in a few places. Do not overbake or the soufflé may be too firm to roll up later.

While roulade bakes, pour the reserved zucchini juice into a 2-cup glass measure with a pouring spout. Add enough whole milk to make $1^{2}/_{3}$ cups, then add the heavy cream. Pour into a small heavy saucepan and heat almost to the boiling point. Melt 2 tablespoons butter in another small heavy saucepan over medium heat. Stir in the flour with a wooden spoon. Cook and stir 2 minutes. Remove pan from heat and whisk in the hot liquid; sauce should be smooth. Return pan to medium-high heat and bring to the boil, whisking constantly. Cook and whisk until thick, about 2 minutes. Remove pan from heat and whisk in remaining 2 tablespoons butter, 1 tablespoon at a time. Season sauce to taste with salt, pepper, and nutmeg.

When the soufflé has settled, sprinkle the top with toasted breadcrumbs. Cover with a sheet of parchment or wax paper with an overhang of about 2 inches at each end. Set a cookie sheet over the soufflé and invert the two. Wait 2 minutes, then lift off the baking pan and carefully remove the wax paper. If you see any brittle edges, cut them off.

Spread the heated vegetables evenly over the soufflé, to the edges. Roll up the soufflé from one of the long sides using the parchment or wax paper to help you. When completely rolled and the seam side is down, transfer the roulade to a serving platter or large board. Cut into 12 slices and place 2 on each dinner plate. Spoon a generous amount of sauce over the slices and serve immediately.

LÉGUMES SOUS UNE COUCHE DU SOUFFLÉ AU FROMAGE
Vegetables under a Cheese Soufflé Blanket

SERVES 6

This dish is the complete package: a mountain of tasty, healthy vegetables beneath a cloud of cheesy soufflé. Here I use broccoli, cauliflower, yellow zucchini, red bell pepper, and onions, but you can use any combination you like or just one favorite vegetable. You will need 2¹/₂ pounds of vegetables in all. All of the components for this distinctive soufflé can be prepared ahead and then it takes only minutes to put them together before baking.

¹/₂ pound broccoli florets

¹/₂ pound cauliflower florets

4 tablespoons olive oil

¹/₂ pound yellow zucchini, cut into ¹/₂-inch dice

1 large yellow onion (8 ounces), cut into ¹/₂-inch dice

1 large red bell pepper, cored, seeded, and cut into ¹/₂-inch dice

2 garlic cloves, chopped

1 teaspoon salt, divided

¹/₂ teaspoon freshly ground black pepper, divided

¹/₂ cup chopped fresh basil

1 tablespoon finely grated lemon zest

2 ounces (¹/₂ cup) finely grated Parmesan

2 ounces (¹/₂ cup) finely grated Pecorino Romano

6 tablespoons unsalted butter, plus more for dish

2 cups whole milk

6 tablespoons all-purpose flour

¹/₄ teaspoon freshly grated nutmeg

¹/₈ teaspoon hot pepper sauce

4 large egg yolks

5 large egg whites, room temperature

Pinch of salt

¹/₄ teaspoon cream of tartar

4 ounces (1 cup) grated Gruyère, Comté or P'tit Basque cheese

Steam the broccoli and cauliflower until crisp-tender, 4 to 5 minutes. Add the vegetables to a bowl of cold water to stop the cooking; drain well. Cut the florets into ¹/₂-inch pieces and pat dry on paper towels.

Heat the olive oil in a large heavy skillet over medium heat. Add the zucchini, onion and bell pepper. Cook until tender, stirring occasionally, 5 to 8 minutes. (It's okay if the vegetables begin to brown a bit.) Stir in the steamed broccoli and cauliflower, and garlic. Season with ¹/₂ teaspoon salt and ¹/₄ teaspoon pepper. Cook about 1 minute to heat vegetables through and stir in the basil and lemon zest. (May be made ahead. Cool, cover, and refrigerate.)

Adjust an oven rack to the lower third position and preheat oven to 400 degrees F. Combine the Parmesan and Pecorino Romano in a small bowl. Butter bottom and sides of a 2 1/2-quart (10 x 2-inch) round baking dish and coat with one-fourth of the mixed cheeses.

Heat milk in small heavy saucepan until bubbling but not boiling; keep warm. Melt 6 tablespoons butter in a large heavy saucepan over medium heat. Stir in the flour with a wooden spoon. Cook and stir 2 minutes. Remove pan from heat and whisk in the hot liquid; sauce should be smooth. Return pan to medium-high heat and bring to the boil, whisking constantly. Cook and whisk until very thick, about 2 minutes. Remove pan from heat. Stir in nutmeg and hot pepper sauce. Season béchamel with remaining 1/2 teaspoon salt and 1/4 teaspoon pepper. Add half of béchamel to the vegetables along with two-thirds of remaining cheese combo and fold gently to blend. Transfer to the prepared baking dish.

Whisk the egg yolks into the remainder of the béchamel in the saucepan. Scrape into a large bowl. Sauce can be tepid to warm when folding in the beaten whites and cheese.

In the bowl of a stand mixer, beat the egg whites with the salt on medium speed until frothy, about 1 minute. Add cream of tartar and beat until soft peaks form. Increase speed to medium-high and beaut until moist stiff peaks form, 1 to 2 minutes. Stir one-fourth of the whites into the béchamel to lighten. Gently fold in remaining whites in two additions along with the Gruyère cheese. Spread the soufflé batter evenly over the vegetables and sprinkle with remaining cheese. (May be made up to 1 hour ahead. Cover with a large upturned pot.) Bake until the soufflé is puffed and dark brown on top, and a skewer inserted into the center comes out clean but moist, 25 to 30 minutes. Serve immediately.

SOUFFLÉS D'ENTREMETS CHAUDS

Hot Dessert Soufflés

You have all been there: the moment when the waiter in a sophisticated restaurant comes to the table and asks if anyone would like to order a hot soufflé for dessert. It is hard to say no to this magical, dramatic creation. The anticipation alone is delicious, but not quite as delicious as the soufflé itself.

You don't have to be in a restaurant to experience the wonder of hot dessert soufflés. You can easily create them at home, and these recipes will get you started. There is everything from simple chocolate, raspberry, lemon or Grand Marnier soufflés; to special occasion vanilla soufflé-filled crêpes; to soufflés flavored with exotic coconut and kaffir lime, passion fruit or huckleberries. Most are made in individual ramekins so you—and each of your guests—can have a hot puffed treat all to yourself.

Hot dessert soufflés are much less intimidating to make than you might think. The reputation that precedes them is most certainly unfounded. And, no, you do not have to make them at the last minute! Believe it or not, the soufflé batter—whether béchamel, bouillie (a cooked paste of flour, milk and butter), egg yolk or fruit—can be made in advance and baked just before serving. That way you can pop them into the oven, pull them out, and serve them at the peak of perfection, just as in a restaurant.

SOUFFLÉS AU CHOCOLAT
Chocolate Soufflés

SERVES 6

These tender, delicate and very chocolaty soufflés are sure crowd-pleasers. Make sure to use a high-quality chocolate for the best flavor. Serve them plain or with Crème Anglaise.

5 tablespoons unsalted butter, plus more for
  ramekins
$1/3$ cup sugar, plus more for ramekins
7 ounces semi-sweet or bittersweet (not
  unsweetened) chocolate, chopped
6 large egg yolks

1 tablespoon vanilla extract
7 large egg whites (scant 1 cup), room temperature
Pinch of salt
$1/4$ teaspoon cream of tartar
Crème Anglaise (page 114)

Adjust an oven rack to the lower third position and preheat the oven to 400 degrees F. Butter the bottoms and sides of six 8-ounce ramekins and coat with sugar. Refrigerate until ready to use.

Melt 5 tablespoons butter and chocolate in medium metal bowl set over a saucepan of simmering water; the bowl should be nestled in the pan but not touch the water. Stir occasionally with a heatproof rubber spatula until the chocolate and butter are melted and smooth. Whisk in the egg yolks two at a time. The chocolate may look granular at first but will become smooth like a thick fudge sauce with continual whisking. Whisk in the vanilla. Remove the bowl from over water; let cool several minutes.

In the bowl of a stand mixer, beat the egg whites and a pinch of salt on medium speed until frothy, about 1 minute. Add cream of tartar and beat until soft peaks form. Gradually beat in $1/3$ cup sugar. Increase speed to medium-high and beat until whites form stiff, shiny peaks, 1 to 2 minutes.

Stir one-fourth of the whites into the chocolate (which may be warm) to lighten. Pile on the remaining whites and fold them in only until no white streaks remain. Divide the batter among prepared ramekins, filling to the rims. Form a "hat" in each soufflé by running a thumb around the inside edge of ramekin to disengage batter from the sides. Space ramekins well apart on a large baking sheet. (Can be prepared up to 2 hours ahead and refrigerated or frozen up to 1 week and thawed 30 minutes.) Bake until the soufflés are puffed and a wooden skewer inserted into the center comes out clean but moist, 10 to 12 minutes. Serve immediately with Crème Anglaise.

Soufflés au Chocolat avec Lait de Noix de Coco et Citron Vert de Kaffir
Chocolate Soufflés with Coconut Milk and Kaffir Lime

SERVES 8

Chocolate, coconut and kaffir lime are combined deliciously in these exotic soufflés. The kaffir lime tree is native to Southeast Asia, and the hourglass-shaped leaves are incorporated into many savory dishes of the cuisines in the region. The surprise is that the leaves work so well in sweet dishes such as this one. The fresh leaves can be frozen up to a few months and used straight from the freezer. Serve these soufflés, which have a light yet pudding-like texture, with Crème Chantilly, a softly whipped cream that barely holds its shape (page 115). For maximum enjoyment, poke a deep hole in the center of the soufflé and spoon in some of the whipped cream.

6 kaffir lime leaves, cut into slivers

1 (14-ounce) can full-fat coconut milk

$1/2$ cup whole milk

3 tablespoons unsalted butter, plus more for
   ramekins

$1/2$ cup sugar, plus more for ramekins

7 ounces bittersweet (not unsweetened) chocolate,
   chopped

$1/3$ cup hot water

$1/3$ cup all-purpose flour

1 teaspoon vanilla extract

$1/4$ teaspoon salt

4 large eggs, separated, room temperature

2 large egg whites ($1/4$ cup), room temperature

Pinch of salt

$1/4$ teaspoon cream of tartar

Crème Chantilly (page 115)

Place the lime leaves in a small heavy saucepan. Add the coconut milk and whole milk and bring liquid to a low boil over low heat. Remove pan from heat, cover, and let stand until milk is completely cool, about 3 hours. Strain into a measuring cup; you should have 2 cups. Discard the lime leaves. (Can be made 1 day ahead. Cover and refrigerate.)

    Adjust an oven rack to the lower third position and preheat the oven to 400 degrees F. Butter the bottoms and sides of eight 1-cup ramekins and coat with sugar. Refrigerate until ready to use.

    Place the chocolate and hot water into a medium metal bowl and set over a saucepan of simmering water; the bowl should not touch the water. Stir occasionally with a whisk until the chocolate is melted, smooth and shiny. Remove bowl from over water.

    Put the flour into a medium heavy saucepan. Gradually pour in the strained milk and whisk until very smooth. Set pan over medium heat and bring liquid to the boil, whisking constantly over the bottom and sides of the pan. Continue boiling 2 minutes, whisking constantly. The sauce will have large thick bubbles. Take pan off the heat. Whisk 3 tablespoons butter, vanilla and salt into the bouillie. Scrape bottom and sides of pan with a heatproof rubber spatula and whisk again to make sure the sauce is perfectly smooth. Whisk in egg yolks one at a time, then whisk in the melted chocolate. Scrape into a large bowl.

In the bowl of a stand mixer, beat the 6 egg whites and a pinch of salt on medium speed until frothy, about 1 minute. Add cream of tartar and beat until soft peaks form. Increase speed to medium-high. Gradually add $^1/_2$ cup sugar and beat until stiff, shiny peaks form, 1 to 2 minutes. Stir one-fourth of the egg whites into the chocolate to lighten. Pile on the remaining whites and fold them in just until no white streaks remain. The soufflé batter will have the consistency of a thick mousse. Divide it among the prepared ramekins, filling to just below rims. Form a "hat" in each soufflé by running a thumb around inside edge of ramekin to disengage batter from the sides. Space ramekins well apart on a large baking sheet. (Can be prepared up to 2 hours ahead and refrigerated or frozen up to 1 week and thawed 30 minutes.) Bake until puffed, with crusty tops, and a wooden skewer inserted into the center comes out clean but moist, 12 to 15 minutes. Serve immediately with Crème Chantilly.

SOUFFLÉS AUX ANANAS
Pineapple Soufflés

SERVES 8

The taste of fresh pineapple shines through in these soufflés. Make sure to pick a perfectly ripe fruit, as pineapple will not get any sweeter after it's picked, only softer. To test for sweetness, hold the base of a room-temperature—not chilled—pineapple to your nose and inhale deeply. A ripe fruit will smell sweet and of pineapple. That is the fruit to select!

2 tablespoons unsalted butter, plus more for ramekins

$^1/_2$ cup sugar, divided, plus more for ramekins

5 ounces fresh pineapple cut into $^1/_4$-inch dice

5 ounces fresh pineapple cut into $^1/_2$-inch pieces

3 tablespoons water

Whole milk, as needed

5 tablespoons all-purpose flour

$^1/_4$ teaspoon salt

4 large egg yolks

1 teaspoon vanilla extract

6 large egg whites ($^3/_4$ cup), room temperature

Pinch of salt

$^1/_4$ teaspoon cream of tartar

Adjust an oven rack to the lower third position and preheat the oven to 400 degrees F. Butter the bottoms and sides of eight 6-ounce ramekins and coat with sugar. Space ramekins well apart on a large baking sheet. Spoon 2 tablespoons diced pineapple into bottom of each ramekin and spread into a single layer. Refrigerate until ready to use.

Put the pineapple pieces into a blender and add the water. Blend to make a smooth purée. Scrape purée into a glass measuring cup; you should have $^2/_3$ to $^3/_4$ cup. Add enough milk to make 1 cup pineapple purée.

Whisk together the flour, $^1/_4$ cup sugar and salt in medium heavy saucepan off heat. Add 2 tablespoons whole milk and whisk to make a smooth, thick, lump-free paste. Gradually whisk in pineapple purée. Set the pan over medium-high heat and bring to the boil, whisking constantly. Continue boiling and whisking for 2 minutes. Remove from heat and whisk in 2 tablespoons butter. Whisk in the egg yolks one at a time. Whisk in vanilla. Return pan to medium heat and cook to thicken the sauce a bit more, whisking constantly, about 1 minute. Cool, whisking occasionally to prevent a skin from forming. (You can make the bouillie base 3 to 4 hours ahead. Cover and refrigerate. Reheat to tepid over low heat, stirring frequently with heatproof rubber spatula, just before whipping egg whites.)

continued >

In the bowl of a stand mixer, beat the egg whites and a pinch of salt on medium speed until frothy, about 1 minute. Add cream of tartar and beat until soft peaks form. Gradually beat in remaining $1/4$ cup sugar. Increase speed to medium-high and beat until the whites form stiff, shiny peaks, 1 to 2 minutes. Stir one-fourth of the egg whites into the sauce base to lighten. Gently fold in remaining whites in two additions only until no white streaks remain.

Divide the batter among prepared ramekins, filling to the rims, then level with a spatula. Form a "hat" in each soufflé by running a thumb around the inside edge of ramekin to disengage batter from the sides. (Can be prepared up to 2 hours ahead. Cover loosely with plastic wrap and refrigerate. To freeze, set in freezer without hats and uncovered until frozen solid, then cover and freeze 1 to 2 days. Thaw 30 minutes, create hats and bake.) Set ramekins well apart on a large baking sheet. Bake until tops of soufflés are nicely browned and have puffed about 2 inches above the rims, and a wooden skewer inserted in center comes out clean but moist, 12 to 15 minutes. Serve immediately.

SOUFFLÉS ST. GERMAIN
AUX ABRICOTS FRAIS
Fresh Apricot St. Germain Soufflés

SERVES 6

I often find that fresh store-bought apricots lack flavor, but cooking them magically frees and transforms the taste locked inside. These creamy soufflés, made with a purée of cooked apricots, sing with the tang of the fruit. St. Germain liqueur, made of elderflowers from the French Alps, adds an alluring note. When apricots are in season, cook up batches of the purée and freeze them to make this soufflé during the winter months.

Unsalted butter for ramekins

$^3/_4$ cup sugar, divided, plus more for ramekins

1 pound fresh apricots, pitted

1 tablespoon freshly squeezed lemon juice

3 tablespoons St. Germain liqueur

5 large egg whites (scant $^2/_3$ cup), room temperature

Pinch of salt

$^1/_4$ teaspoon cream of tartar

Butter the bottom and sides of six 6-ounce ramekins and coat with sugar. Refrigerate.

Purée the apricots in a food processor until smooth, about 1 minute. Combine purée and lemon juice in a medium heavy nonreactive saucepan, and cook over medium to medium-high heat, stirring almost constantly with a wooden spoon, until very thick and reduced to $^3/_4$ cup, about 15 minutes. Remove pan from heat. Stir in $^1/_2$ cup sugar. Return pan to medium heat and cook, stirring constantly, until the purée is the consistency of soft jam, about 5 minutes. Scrape into a large bowl; cool completely. Stir in the liqueur.

Adjust an oven rack to the lower third position and preheat the oven to 400 degrees F.

In the bowl of a stand mixer, beat the egg whites and a pinch of salt on medium speed until frothy, about 1 minute. Add cream of tartar and beat until soft peaks form. Beat in remaining $^1/_4$ cup sugar 1 tablespoon at a time, and continue beating until stiff, shiny peaks form, about 1 to 2 minutes.

Stir about one-fourth of the egg whites into apricot base until almost combined. Pile on remaining whites and fold them in only until no white streaks remain. Divide among prepared ramekins, filling to the rims, and level with a spatula. (Can be prepared up to 2 hours ahead and refrigerated, or frozen for up to 1 week and thawed 30 minutes.)

When ready to bake, unwrap and let stand at room temperature 30 minutes. Bake 10 to 12 minutes, until tops of soufflés are flecked with brown, and the tip of a wooden skewer inserted into the center comes out clean but moist. Serve immediately.

Soufflés aux Framboises Fraîches

Fresh Raspberry Soufflés

SERVES 6

In these simple hot raspberry soufflés the color stays an appealing pink. The base, made with egg whites but no egg yolks, is thickened with cornstarch and flavored with Chambord, a raspberry liqueur. This is one of the best fruit soufflés I know.

Unsalted butter, room temperature, for ramekins

$^1/_2$ cup sugar, divided, plus more for ramekins

12 ounces fresh raspberries

1 tablespoon plus 2 teaspoons cornstarch

$^1/_8$ teaspoon salt

2 tablespoons Chambord liqueur

4 large egg whites ($^1/_2$ cup), room temperature

Pinch of salt

$^1/_4$ teaspoon cream of tartar

Adjust an oven rack to the lower third position and preheat the oven to 400 degrees F. Butter the bottoms and sides of six 6-ounce ramekins and coat with sugar. Refrigerate until ready to use.

Purée the raspberries in a food processor. Pass through a fine-mesh strainer to remove the seeds and put the purée into a medium heavy nonreactive saucepan. Whisk in $^1/_4$ cup sugar, cornstarch, and salt. Set pan over medium heat and bring purée to the boil, stirring constantly along the bottom and sides of the pan with a heatproof rubber spatula, until purée is thick, 1 to 2 minutes. Remove from heat and scrape down sides of pan. Add Chambord to the purée, but do not stir to prevent a skin from forming. Cool completely, then stir.

In the bowl of a stand mixer, beat the egg whites and a pinch of salt on medium speed until frothy, about 1 minute. Add cream of tartar and beat until soft peaks form. With mixer going, beat in remaining $^1/_4$ cup sugar 1 tablespoon at a time, waiting a few seconds between additions. Increase speed to medium-high and beat until the whites form stiff, shiny peaks, 1 to 2 minutes. Stir one-fourth of the egg whites into the raspberry base to lighten. Add the base to the remaining beaten whites and fold gently only until no white streaks remain.

Divide the batter among prepared ramekins, filling to the rims, and level with a spatula. Form a "hat" in each soufflé by running a thumb around inside edge of ramekin to disengage batter from the sides. Space ramekins well apart on a large baking sheet. (Can be prepared 2 hours ahead. Cover and refrigerate, or freeze 1 to 2 days. Unwrap and thaw 30 minutes at room temperature before baking.)

Bake 10 to 12 minutes, until the soufflés are well puffed, the tops are tinged with brown, and a wooden skewer inserted into the center comes out clean but moist. Serve immediately.

Soufflés au Citron de Meyer
Meyer Lemon Soufflés

SERVES 6

Meyer lemons, identified in 1908 by Frank N. Meyer, are believed to be a cross between Eureka or Lisbon lemons and mandarin oranges. They are less acidic than other lemons and have a sweeter and more floral taste. When cut into, the fruit can even have a slightly orange tint. Much of the flavor of a Meyer lemon is in its thin skin, which is not as bitter as that of a regular lemon. These soufflés contain both the zest and juice of the fruit for a double punch of lemon flavor.

Unsalted butter, for ramekins

³/₄ cup sugar, divided, plus more for ramekins

6 large eggs, separated, room temperature

4 tablespoons freshly squeezed Meyer lemon juice

2 tablespoons finely grated Meyer lemon zest

Pinch of salt

¹/₄ teaspoon cream of tartar

Adjust an oven rack to the lower third position and preheat the oven to 375 degrees F. Butter the bottoms and sides of six 1-cup ramekins and coat with sugar. Refrigerate until ready to use.

Put the egg yolks into a medium bowl and start beating them on medium speed using a hand-held electric mixer. Gradually beat in ¹/₂ cup sugar and continue beating until yolks are thick and pale yellow and form a slowly dissolving ribbon (see page 16) when the beaters are lifted, about 5 minutes. Beat in the juice and zest.

In a clean bowl with clean beaters, beat the egg whites and a pinch of salt on medium speed until frothy, about 1 minute. Add cream of tartar and beat until soft peaks form. Beat in remaining ¹/₄ cup sugar 1 tablespoon at a time, waiting about 10 seconds between additions, and continue beating until the whites form stiff, shiny peaks, 1 to 2 minutes.

Pour the yolks over the beaten whites and fold them together gently and thoroughly only until no white streaks remain. Divide the batter among prepared ramekins, filling to the rims. Form a "hat" in each soufflé by running a thumb around the inside edge of ramekin to disengage batter from the sides. Space ramekins well apart on a large baking sheet. (Can be prepared up to 2 hours ahead and refrigerated, or frozen for up to 1 week and thawed 30 minutes.) Bake until the soufflés are puffed, the tops are tinged with brown, and a wooden skewer inserted into the center comes out clean but moist. Serve immediately.

SOUFFLÉS AU CARAMEL
Caramel Soufflés

SERVES 6

In these elegant soufflés, a true caramel is added to the creamy base for the ultimate in caramel flavor. To make things even more luscious, serve with Crème Anglaise.

Butter for ramekins

1 cup plus 2 tablespoons sugar, divided, plus more
 for ramekins

1 cup whole milk

1/2 cup heavy cream

2 tablespoons cornstarch

1 tablespoon all-purpose flour

1/4 teaspoon salt

4 large egg yolks

2 teaspoons vanilla extract

8 large egg whites (1 cup), room temperature

Pinch of salt

1/2 teaspoon cream of tartar

Crème Anglaise (page 114; optional)

Butter bottoms and sides of six 8-ounce ramekins and coat with sugar. Refrigerate until ready to use.

Combine the milk and cream in a small heavy saucepan and bring to a simmer over medium heat. Keep hot over very low heat.

Put ¾ cup sugar into a medium heavy skillet, preferably stainless steel or enameled cast iron so you can see the color of the caramel as the sugar melts. Set skillet over medium heat and leave sugar undisturbed until it begins to melt into a pale-colored syrup around the edges; this will take several minutes. At that point, stir with a wooden spoon occasionally as the sugar melts completely into a deep, dark caramel color. The caramel must be dark or it will have no taste. There may be wisps of smoke, but do not allow caramel to burn. Remove skillet from heat and immediately and slowly add the hot milk and cream; the caramel will seethe and sputter. Return skillet to medium heat and cook, stirring frequently, until caramel has remelted and the liquid has the color of café au lait. Take skillet off the heat.

Stir together the cornstarch, flour and salt in a small bowl. Put the egg yolks and 2 table-spoons sugar into the bowl of a stand mixer and beat on medium speed until thick and pale and a ribbon forms when the beater is raised. Add the dry ingredients and beat on low speed until incorporated. With the mixer on low, beat in the hot caramel liquid 1 tablespoon at a time. After about half has been added, beat in remaining liquid, adding in a thin stream.

Scrape the caramel base into a medium heavy saucepan set over medium heat. Bring to the boil, whisking constantly over the bottom and sides of the pan. Switch to a heatproof spatula to prevent the sauce base from sticking and burning, and boil 2 to 3 minutes, stirring constantly. Take pan off heat, stir in vanilla, and scrape the caramel base into a large bowl. Press a round of wax or parchment paper directly onto the surface to prevent a skin from forming. Let the caramel base cool to room temperature.

Adjust an oven rack to the lower third position and preheat the oven to 400 degrees F.

In the bowl of a stand mixer, beat the egg whites and a pinch of salt on medium speed until frothy, about 1 minute. Add cream of tartar and beat until soft peaks form. Beat in 4 tablespoons granulated sugar 1 tablespoon at a time. Increase speed to medium-high and beat until the whites form stiff, shiny peaks, 1 to 2 minutes.

Whisk the caramel base until completely smooth. Add one-fourth of the whites and whisk to lighten. Add remaining whites in two additions, folding until no white streaks remain. Divide the batter among prepared ramekins, filling to about ¼ inch below the rims. Form a "hat" in each souf-flé by running a thumb around the inside edge of ramekin to disengage batter from the sides. Space ramekins well apart on a large baking sheet. (Can be prepared 2 hours ahead and refrigerated or frozen up to 1 week and thawed 30 minutes.) Bake about 15 minutes, until puffed and set and a wooden skewer inserted into the center comes out clean but moist. Serve immediately. Make a hole with a dessert spoon and pour in the Crème Anglaise.

Soufflés au Grand Marnier
Grand Marnier Soufflés

SERVES 6 OR 8

This is one of the most famous and popular dessert soufflés. It is light and airy yet surprisingly creamy, with a pronounced flavor of orange from the liqueur, Grand Marnier.

2 tablespoons unsalted butter, plus more for ramekins

$^1/_2$ sugar, divided, plus more for ramekins

4 tablespoons all-purpose flour

$^1/_4$ teaspoon salt

1 cup cold whole milk

3 tablespoons Grand Marnier or other orange-flavored liqueur

5 large eggs separated, room temperature

Pinch of salt

$^1/_4$ teaspoon cream of tartar

Adjust an oven rack to the lower third position and preheat the oven to 400 degrees F. Butter the bottoms and sides of six 1-cup or eight 6-ounce ramekins and coat with sugar. Refrigerate.

Whisk together $^1/_4$ cup of the sugar, the flour, and salt in a medium heavy saucepan. Whisk in $^1/_4$ cup of the milk to make a smooth paste, then whisk in remaining milk. Set pan over medium heat and bring bouillie to the boil, stirring constantly along the bottom and sides of pan with a heatproof rubber spatula; the mixture will be thick. Switch to a whisk and continue boiling about 3 minutes, until the sauce is pasty looking. Remove pan from heat and whisk in butter. Whisk in egg yolks one at a time. Scrape the base into a large bowl and film with the liqueur. Set aside.

In the bowl of a stand mixer, beat the egg whites and a pinch of salt on medium speed until frothy, about 1 minute. Add cream of tartar and continue beating until soft peaks form. Gradually beat in remaining $^1/_4$ cup sugar about 1 tablespoon at a time, waiting a few seconds between additions. Increase speed to medium-high and continue beating until the whites form stiff, shiny peaks, 1 to 2 minutes.

Whisk the sauce base to incorporate the Grand Marnier. Stir in one-fourth of the whites to lighten. Pile on remaining whites and fold in gently only until no white streaks remain. Divide the batter among prepared ramekins, filling to just below the rims. Form a "hat" in each soufflé by running a thumb around the inside edge of ramekin to disengage batter from the sides. *Note:* This batter is soft and the "hat" will disappear. (Can be prepared 2 hours ahead and refrigerated or frozen up to 1 week and thawed 30 minutes.) Space ramekins well apart on a large baking sheet. Bake until soufflés are puffed and browned on top and a wooden skewer inserted into center comes out clean but moist, 10 to 12 minutes. Serve immediately.

SOUFFLÉS AU CAFÉ
Coffee Soufflés

SERVES 6

This is a must-have soufflé for coffee lovers. The intense flavor comes from steeping whole coffee beans in hot milk. Use light, medium or dark-roasted beans—but not flavored beans—for optimum taste. The coffee-infused milk becomes part of the base of this high-rising soufflé with a light velvety texture. Serve with Crème Chantilly and/or Sauce au Chocolat.

2 tablespoons unsalted butter, plus more for ramekins

$1/2$ cup sugar, divided, plus more for ramekins

1 cup whole milk, plus more as needed

$1/2$ cup whole unflavored coffee beans

5 tablespoons all-purpose flour

$1/4$ teaspoon salt

4 large egg yolks

1 teaspoon vanilla extract

6 large egg whites ($3/4$ cup), room temperature

Pinch of salt

$1/4$ teaspoon cream of tartar

Confectioners' or superfine sugar, for garnish

Crème Chantilly (page 115; optional)

Sauce au Chocolat (page 120; optional)

Butter bottoms and sides of six 6-ounce ramekins and coat with sugar. Refrigerate until ready to use.

Combine milk and coffee beans in a small heavy saucepan over medium heat and bring to the boil. Stir, remove pan from heat and cover. Let sit 30 minutes. Strain milk into a glass measuring cup; you should have about $3/4$ cup. Add enough additional milk to make 1 cup.

Whisk the flour, $1/4$ cup sugar, and salt in a medium heavy saucepan off heat. Whisk in $1/4$ cup coffee milk to make a thick, lump-free paste. Gradually add remaining coffee milk, whisking until smooth. Set pan over medium-high heat and bring to the boil, whisking constantly. Continue boiling and whisking until very thick and bubbly, 2 to 3 minutes. Lift pan off heat occasionally to make sure the bouillie is not sticking to the pan. Off heat, whisk in 2 tablespoons butter. Scrape the base into a medium bowl and whisk in the egg yolks two at a time, then vanilla. Let cool slightly, whisking occasionally to prevent a skin from forming; the base may be warm when completing soufflé.

Adjust an oven rack to the lower third position and preheat the oven to 400 degrees F.

In the bowl of a stand mixer, beat the egg whites and a pinch of salt on medium speed until frothy, about 1 minute. Add cream of tartar and beat until soft peaks form. Gradually beat in

continued >

remaining $^{1}/_{4}$ cup sugar. Increase speed to medium-high and continue beating until the whites form stiff, shiny peaks. Whisk one-fourth of the whites into the coffee base to lighten. Gently fold in remaining whites until no white streaks remain.

Divide the soufflé batter among prepared ramekins. Form a "hat" in each soufflé by running a thumb around the inside edge of ramekin to disengage batter from the sides. (Can be prepared 2 hours ahead or frozen up to 1 week and thawed 30 minutes.) Space ramekins well apart on a large baking sheet. Dust tops of soufflés very lightly with confectioners' or superfine sugar. Bake until puffed and browned, about 13 minutes. Serve immediately, passing Crème Chantilly and/or Sauce au Chocolat separately.

SOUFFLÉS DE CRÊPES À LA VANILLE
Vanilla Crêpes Soufflés

SERVES 6

Here is an elegant dessert that can be assembled in minutes for a special-occasion dinner, as most of the components can be made ahead. Large crêpes, which you need to make ahead, are filled with a vanilla soufflé made from a pastry cream and baked for a few minutes. The souffléd crêpes, which puff magnificently, are complemented by a bittersweet Sauce au Chocolat. Both the crêpes and chocolate sauce can be made a day or two ahead.

Pastry Cream

1 cup whole milk

3 large egg yolks

4 tablespoons sugar, divided

2 tablespoons all-purpose flour

1¹/₂ teaspoons cornstarch

¹/₈ teaspoon salt

¹/₄–¹/₂ teaspoon vanilla bean paste or
   2 teaspoons vanilla extract

Soufflé and Finishing

4 large egg whites (¹/₂ cup), room temperature

Pinch of salt

2 tablespoons sugar

¹/₄ teaspoon cream of tartar

6 large Crêpes (page 116) 7 to 8 inches in
   diameter, room temperature

2 tablespoons unsalted butter, melted

Confectioners' sugar, for garnish

Sauce au Chocolat (page 120), room temperature

Fresh raspberries or sliced strawberries (optional)

For the pastry cream, bring milk to the boil in a small heavy saucepan over medium heat; do not let it bubble over. Keep milk hot. Put the egg yolks into a medium bowl and beat with a hand-held electric mixer on medium speed until they begin to thicken, about 1 minute. Gradually add 2 tablespoons sugar, raise speed to medium-high, and continue beating until the yolks are thick and pale, 3 to 5 minutes more. On low speed, beat in the flour, cornstarch, and salt. Add 2 table-spoons sugar to the hot milk and stir to dissolve. With the mixer on low, slowly add milk to the egg yolks and continue beating until smooth. Using a rubber spatula, scrape the bowl to make sure the pastry cream is thoroughly blended. Transfer pastry cream base to the milk saucepan. Set pan over medium-high heat and bring to the boil, whisking constantly. Continue boiling and whisking until thickened, about 2 minutes. Scrape pastry cream into a medium bowl and whisk in the vanilla paste or extract. Press a round of wax or parchment paper directly onto the surface to prevent a skin from forming.

continued >

Adjust an oven rack to the lower third position and preheat the oven to 375 degrees F.

In the bowl of a stand mixer, beat the egg whites and a pinch of salt on medium speed until frothy, about 1 minute. Add cream of tartar and beat until soft peaks form. Gradually beat in 2 tablespoons sugar, increase speed to medium-high, and beat until the whites form stiff, shiny peaks, 1 to 2 minutes. Whisk one-fourth of the egg whites into the pastry cream to lighten. Pile on remaining whites and fold in only until no white streaks remain.

Lightly butter a 17 x 12 x 1-inch rimmed baking sheet. With a long side facing you, drape one crêpe with its best side facing down over upper left edge of the sheet so that half of the crêpe is resting on sheet and other half is hanging over edge. Spoon one-sixth of the soufflé batter in a strip on the part of the crêpe resting on the sheet, and fold remaining half of the crêpe over the soufflé to cover it and make a half-moon shape.

Set another crêpe with best side facing down over the filled crêpe so that half of the crêpe rests on the soufflé-filled crêpe and the other half rests on the sheet. Spoon one-fifth of the remaining soufflé batter in a strip on the part of the crêpe resting on the baking sheet, and fold the unfilled portion of crêpe over the soufflé as before to make another half-moon shape. At this point you'll have two filled crêpes on the left side of the baking sheet. Repeat these instructions to make 2 filled crêpes down the center of the pan and 2 on the right side of the pan. The baking sheet will have two long rows of 3 crêpes each. Brush with melted butter and dust with confectioners' sugar.

Bake until the soufflé filling is puffed and set. Using a large metal spatula, transfer each crêpe soufflé to a dessert plate. Dust crêpes again with confectioners' sugar and drizzle with Sauce au Chocolat. Add a few berries, if you like. Serve immediately.

SOUFFLÉ FLAMBÉ AU CITRON ET AMARETTO ET AUX AMARETTI
Flaming Lemon Amaretto-Amaretti Soufflé

SERVES 6

For sheer drama, there's nothing like a soufflé flambé, and this one, flavored with fresh lemon and almond liqueur, is sure to impress. To garner the biggest reaction, make sure your guests are seated at the table and the lights are turned off when you ignite the soufflé. Serve it with Crème Anglaise mixed with Crème de Citron.

Butter for ramekins

6 double amaretti cookies, 3 finely crushed and 3 broken into $^1/_4$-inch pieces

10 tablespoons sugar, divided

Finely grated zest of 2 large lemons

6 large egg yolks

Salt

$^1/_2$ cup amaretto liqueur, divided

6 large egg whites ($^3/_4$ cup), room temperature

$^1/_4$ teaspoon cream of tartar

Crème de Citron (page 118)

Crème Anglaise (page 114)

Confectioners' sugar, for garnish

Adjust an oven rack to the lower third position and preheat the oven to 375 degrees F.

Butter a $2^1/_2$-quart round baking dish 10 inches in diameter and 2 inches deep or a similar-sized oval baking dish. Dust bottom and sides of the pan with the finely crushed amaretti cookies.

Using a mortar with pestle, pound $^1/_2$ cup sugar and lemon zest together to extract as much lemon oil as possible. Alternatively, blend $^1/_2$ cup sugar and lemon zest together in a spice grinder for about 30 seconds. Or, using a fork, mash $^1/_2$ cup sugar and the lemon zest to a paste in a bowl.

Beat the egg yolks and a pinch of salt in a medium bowl with a hand-held electric mixer on medium speed until slightly thickened, about 1 minute. Gradually beat in the lemon sugar with zest, and continue beating until yolks are pale and thick and form a ribbon when the beater is raised, 3 to 5 minutes more. Beat in $^1/_4$ cup amaretto liqueur. Scrape the yolks into a medium heavy saucepan and set over medium heat. Whisk until yolks are thick and form a ribbon when the whisk is raised, 3 to 4 minutes. Do not allow yolks to boil. Remove pan from heat and beat on medium speed with a hand-held electric mixer until yolks are cool and very thick, about 5 minutes.

In the large bowl of a stand mixer, beat the whites and a pinch of salt on medium speed until frothy, about 1 minute. Add cream of tartar and beat until soft peaks form. Add remaining

continued >

2 tablespoons sugar, increase speed to medium-high, and beat until the whites form stiff, shiny peaks, 1 to 2 minutes. Stir one-fourth of the whites into the cooled yolk mixture to lighten. Pile on remaining whites and fold in until no white streaks remain.

Gently spread half the soufflé batter on the bottom of prepared baking dish; do not deflate the batter. Sprinkle with the broken amaretti pieces. Top with remaining soufflé batter, spreading carefully. (Can be prepared 2 hours ahead. Cover with an inverted pot and let stand at room temperature. Preheat oven 30 minutes before serving.) Bake until soufflé is puffed and evenly browned on top and a wooden skewer inserted into the center comes out clean but moist, 20 to 25 minutes.

Meanwhile, stir ¼ cup Crème de Citron into Crème Anglaise in a medium bowl. Transfer the sauce to a serving pitcher.

Heat remaining ¼ cup amaretto liqueur in a small heavy saucepan over low heat just until warm. Bring heated liqueur and just-baked soufflé to the table and place on trivets. Pour liqueur over the soufflé and ignite with a match. After flames have subsided, divide soufflé among serving bowls. Pass the sauce separately.

SOUFFLÉS AUX MYRTILLES
Huckleberry Soufflés

SERVES 6

Wild huckleberries are the jewels of summer in the western Rocky Mountains, where I live. Although related to blueberries, huckleberries are tangier and more assertive than their cousins. The best substitute for the huckleberry is the wild Maine blueberry, but, really, any blueberry will do. There are no egg yolks in this light yet flavorful soufflé.

Unsalted butter for ramekins

10 tablespoons sugar, divided, plus more for ramekins

2 cups (10 ounces) fresh or thawed frozen huckleberries or blueberries

1 tablespoon fresh lime juice

2^1/$_2$ teaspoons cornstarch

Salt

4 large egg whites (^{1}/$_2$ cup), room temperature

^{1}/$_4$ teaspoon cream of tartar

Butter bottoms and sides of six 6-ounce ramekins and coat with sugar. Refrigerate until ready to use.

Combine the huckleberries and ^{1}/$_2$ cup sugar in a small heavy saucepan over very low heat. Cover and cook until berries have released their juices, about 25 minutes. Remove the cover, stir berries and cook until syrupy, about 5 minutes. Set a strainer over a glass measuring cup. Pour berries into the strainer and press with a wooden spoon to extract as much juice as possible; you should have about ^{2}/$_3$ cup. Return juice to the saucepan. Stir lime juice, cornstarch, and a pinch of salt together in a small bowl; then stir into the huckleberry juice. Set pan over medium heat and cook, stirring almost constantly with a heatproof rubber spatula, for 2 to 3 minutes, until juice boils and thickens. Cool to room temperature.

Adjust an oven rack to the lower third position and preheat the oven to 400 degrees F.

In the bowl of a stand mixer, beat the egg whites and a pinch of salt on medium speed until frothy, about 1 minute. Add cream of tartar and beat until soft peaks form. Beat in remaining 2 tablespoons sugar 1 tablespoon at a time. Increase speed to medium-high and continue beating until the whites form stiff, shiny peaks, 1 to 2 minutes more.

Scrape the cool huckleberry sauce over the beaten whites and gently fold together until no white streaks remain. Divide soufflé batter among prepared ramekins, filling to the rims. Form a "hat" in each soufflé by running a thumb around the inside edge of ramekin to disengage batter from the sides. (Can be prepared 2 hours ahead and refrigerated or frozen for 1 week and thawed 30 minutes.) Space ramekins well apart on a large baking sheet. Bake until soufflés are puffed, tinged with brown on the top, and a wooden skewer inserted into the center comes out clean but moist, about 10 minutes. Serve immediately.

Soufflés aux Fraises Fraîches
Fresh Strawberry Soufflés

SERVES 2

Sometimes there is nothing quite like a beautiful hot strawberry soufflé after a romantic dinner for two. It's best to use small farmers market berries—preferably organic—as they have more flavor and less moisture than the supermarket varieties. If you wish, accompany the soufflés with glasses of a sweet dessert wine such as Moscato, late-harvest Riesling or Sauternes. This recipe is also perfect for company and can easily be doubled or tripled.

Butter for ramekins

5–7 tablespoons sugar, divided, plus more for ramekins

10 ounces fresh strawberries, washed and stemmed (6 ounces left whole, 4 ounces thinly sliced)

1 1/2 teaspoons cornstarch

Salt

1 tablespoon Grand Marnier or other orange liqueur (optional)

3 large egg whites, room temperature

1/8 teaspoon cream of tartar

Butter the bottoms and sides of two 1-cup ramekins and coat with sugar. Refrigerate until ready to use.

Combine the whole berries, 2 tablespoons sugar, cornstarch and a pinch of salt in a food processor and pulse until berries are chopped into very small pieces, about five 1-second pulses. Scrape berries into a small heavy saucepan set over medium heat and cook, stirring constantly with a heatproof rubber spatula, until thick and bubbly, about 5 minutes. Take pan off the heat and cool berries completely. (This step may be done hours ahead. Cover and refrigerate. Bring to room temperature when ready to bake soufflés.)

Combine the sliced berries, 1 to 2 tablespoons sugar to taste, and liqueur, if using, in a small bowl. Cover and refrigerate until ready to use.

Adjust an oven rack to the lower third position and preheat the oven to 400 degrees F.

In the bowl of a stand mixer, beat the egg whites and a pinch of salt on medium speed until frothy, about 1 minute. Add cream of tartar and beat until soft peaks form. Add remaining 3 tablespoons sugar 1 tablespoon at a time. Increase speed to medium-high and beat until the whites form stiff, shiny peaks, 1 to 2 minutes more.

Gently fold the cooled cooked strawberry purée into the whites until no white streaks remain. Divide the soufflé batter between prepared ramekins, filling to the rims, and smooth the tops with a spatula. Form a "hat" in each soufflé by running a thumb around the inside edge of ramekin to disengage batter from the sides. (Can be prepared 2 hours ahead and refrigerated or frozen up to 1 week and thawed 30 minutes.) Space ramekins well apart on a baking sheet. Bake until the soufflés have puffed about 2 inches above the rims and a wooden skewer inserted into the center comes out clean but moist, 10 to 12 minutes. Serve immediately with the cold strawberry sauce.

Soufflés Chauds au Fruit de la Passiflore
Hot Passion Fruit Soufflés

SERVES 6

Passion fruit, a tropical fruit that grows on a vine, has an exquisite tart flavor that is quite captivating. The taste is incomparable and indescribable and must be experienced firsthand. Fortunately, bottled passion fruit juice or purée can be purchased online, and both keep for months. This simple and extremely light soufflé has only three major ingredients—eggs, sugar and passion fruit juice—allowing the exotic fruit flavor to shine through. Without a stabilizing base, the proper beating of yolks and whites becomes more important than ever in this soufflé.

Unsalted butter for ramekins

12 tablespoons sugar, divided, plus more for ramekins

6 large eggs, separated, room temperature

Salt

1/4 teaspoon cream of tartar

6 tablespoons passion fruit juice*

Butter the bottoms and sides of six 8-ounce ramekins and coat with sugar. Refrigerate until ready to use.

Adjust an oven rack to the lower third position and preheat the oven to 400 degrees F.

Put the egg yolks and a pinch of salt in a large bowl. Using a hand-held electric mixer, beat on medium speed until eggs just begin to thicken, about 1 minute. Increase speed to medium-high and, while beating, gradually add 6 tablespoons sugar. Continue beating until the yolks are very thick, pale yellow in color and form a ribbon when the beater is raised, about 5 minutes. This step is critical; so do not skimp on beating.

In the bowl of a stand mixer, beat the whites and a pinch of salt on medium speed until frothy, about 1 minute. Add cream of tartar and beat until soft peaks form. While beating, gradually add remaining 6 tablespoons sugar. Increase speed to medium-high, and continue beating until the whites form stiff, shiny peaks, 1 to 2 minutes more.

Whisk the passion fruit juice into the beaten yolks. Add one-fourth of the whites and whisk to lighten. Fold in remaining whites in two batches until no white streaks remain. The soufflé batter should have the texture of softly whipped cream.

Divide the soufflé batter among prepared ramekins, filling to rims. If the filling domes a bit in the center, that's fine. Form a "hat" in each soufflé by running a thumb around inside edge of

continued >

ramekin to disengage batter from the sides. (Can be prepared 2 hours ahead and refrigerated or frozen up to 1 week and thawed 30 minutes.) Space ramekins well apart on a baking sheet. Bake until the soufflés have puffed 2 inches above the rims, the tops are nicely browned, and a wooden skewer inserted into the center comes out clean but moist, 10 to 13 minutes. Serve immediately.

*I recommend the Aunty Lilikoi brand, http://www.auntylilikoi.com/syrups-and-juices/unsweetened-passion-fruit-juice.html. Toll-free telephone orders: 866-545-4564; address 9875 Waimea Road, Waimea, Kauai, Hawaii 96796.

SOUFFLÉ ROTHSCHILD
Soufflé Rothschild

SERVES 6

The original version of this soufflé, created by the founder of classic French cookery, Marie-Antonin Carême (1784–1833), for Jacob de Rothschild, included real gold flakes. But this elegant soufflé, filled with Kirsch-soaked candied fruit, is so beautiful and delicious that gold is superfluous. However, a sauce of chilled Crème Anglaise is a welcome addition.

4 ounces total of 3 different candied fruits (e.g., cherries, pineapple, apricots, orange rind, lemon rind, pears, and citron), finely chopped with a large chef's knife

3 tablespoons Kirsch

2 tablespoons unsalted butter, plus more for mold

6 tablespoons sugar, divided, plus more for mold

3 tablespoons all-purpose flour

Salt

$^3/_4$ cup whole milk

4 large egg yolks

1 teaspoon vanilla extract

6 large egg whites ($^3/_4$ cup), room temperature

$^1/_4$ teaspoon cream of tartar

Superfine sugar, for garnish

Crème Anglaise (page 114; optional)

Combine the chopped candied fruit and Kirsch in a small bowl. Cover and let stand for 1 hour or up to 3 days.

Butter a 6-cup charlotte mold ($6^1/_2$ inches in diameter by 4 inches high) or an 8-cup ceramic soufflé dish (7 inches in diameter by $3^1/_4$ inches high). Coat the mold or dish completely with sugar. Refrigerate until ready to use.

Adjust an oven rack to the lower third position and preheat the oven to 400 degrees F.

Whisk together 4 tablespoons sugar, the flour and a pinch of salt in a 3-quart heavy saucepan. Add $^1/_4$ cup milk and whisk to form a thick, lump-free paste. Whisk in remaining $^1/_2$ cup milk. Set pan over medium heat and bring to the boil, stirring constantly with a heatproof spatula, making sure to scrape all over the bottom and sides. Continue boiling 2 minutes, stirring constantly. Remove pan from heat and whisk in the 2 tablespoons butter until smooth. Add the egg yolks 1 at a time, whisking well after each addition. Beat in vanilla. Set soufflé base aside.

In the bowl of a stand mixer, beat the egg whites and a pinch of salt on medium speed until frothy, about 1 minute. Add cream of tartar and beat until soft peaks form. Gradually add remaining 2 tablespoons sugar. Increase speed to medium-high, and beat until the whites form stiff, shiny peaks, 1 to 2 minutes more.

continued >

Whisk the soufflé base until smooth. Stir in the dried fruits and liqueur. Stir in one-fourth of the whites to lighten. Gently fold in remaining whites in two additions, folding only until no white streaks remain. Transfer batter to prepared mold or dish and set on a large baking sheet. (You can prepare the soufflé batter up to 2 hours ahead, transfer it to the charlotte mold or other baking dish, and cover it with an upturned bowl or large pot. When ready to bake, preheat the oven for 30 minutes.) Place in the oven and immediately reduce oven temperature to 375 degrees F. Bake 20 minutes. Reach into the oven and sprinkle the top of soufflé with superfine sugar. Continue baking until soufflé has risen considerably, its top is nicely browned, and a wooden skewer inserted into the center comes out clean but moist, 10 to 15 minutes more. Serve immediately.

CHAPTER 3

SOUFFLÉS D'ENTREMETS FROIDS
Cold Dessert Soufflés

Technically speaking, a cold soufflé is a mousse. It's an airy, sweet dessert molded in a large soufflé dish wrapped with a paper collar to extend the height of the dish. The mousse is poured into the dish, rises above the rim into the area of the collar, and is either refrigerated or frozen to set it. At serving time the collar is peeled away, revealing what looks like a very tall soufflé. It's dramatic, and the advantage is that it is made ahead of time.

You have more flexibility with a cold soufflé than with a hot one. When hot, a soufflé has to be eaten immediately. A cold soufflé allows you to linger over dessert and be more flexible with it.

Cold soufflés may be unmolded, cut into portions, and served with various sauces. They make excellent plated desserts, as in the Almond Praline Soufflé Floating Islands (page 102).

The Bittersweet Chocolate Roulade Soufflé (page 99) starts out as a hot soufflé baked in a sheet pan, but it is allowed to cool completely before being rolled around a filling of flavored whipped cream.

For a dessert that's all ready and waiting, a cold soufflé makes a good choice.

GÂTEAU DU SOUFFLÉ AU CHOCOLAT TOMBÉ
Fallen Chocolate Soufflé Cake

8 SERVINGS

This is a soufflé—a cake actually—that is meant to fall before serving. How much fun is that? It's similar to a soufflé batter but contains a goodly amount of butter and some ground almonds, which makes it heavier than traditional soufflé formulas. It is moist and chocolaty, somewhat like a pudding, and quite irresistible. You'll beam with pleasure watching it sink slowly in its pan as it cools. Serve portions with very cold Crème Anglaise (page 114) or Crème Chantilly (page 115).

8 ounces bittersweet chocolate, chopped

8 tablespoons (1 stick) unsalted butter, cut into pieces, plus more for pan

2 teaspoons vanilla extract

4 large eggs, separated

$^1/_2$ cup sugar, divided

$^1/_4$ teaspoon salt

$^1/_4$ cup ($^3/_4$ ounce) finely ground almonds or almond meal

$^1/_4$ teaspoon cream of tartar

Crème Anglaise (page 114) or lightly sweetened Crème Chantilly (page 115)

Adjust an oven rack to the center position and preheat the oven to 325 degrees F. Butter an 8-inch springform pan and line the bottom with parchment or wax paper; butter the paper.

Put the chocolate and butter into a metal bowl and set the bowl into a large skillet with about 1 inch of simmering water. Stir occasionally with a wooden spoon or rubber spatula until the chocolate and butter are melted and smooth. Remove bowl from the water and stir in vanilla.

In a medium bowl, start beating the egg yolks on medium speed with a hand-held electric mixer. Gradually add $^1/_4$ cup of the sugar, beating several seconds between additions. Increase speed to medium-high and continue beating for 3 to 5 minutes more, until yolks are very thick and pale and form a slowly dissolving ribbon when the beater is raised. Beat in the salt and almonds. Fold yolks into the chocolate, but don't be too thorough; it's okay if you see streaks of yolk.

In a clean bowl and using clean beaters, beat the egg whites on medium speed until frothy, about 1 minute. Add the cream of tartar and beat until the whites form soft peaks. While beating, gradually add the remaining $^1/_4$ cup sugar about 1 tablespoon at a time, beating a few seconds between additions. Raise speed to medium-high and continue beating until the whites form stiff, shiny peaks that hold a point.

continued >

Stir about one-fourth of the whites into the chocolate, and fold in remaining whites gently until no whites show. Scrape the batter into prepared pan and spread level very gently; pan will be about half full. Put into the oven.

During baking the soufflé cake will rise right to the top of the pan. The center of the cake may look underdone. Bake until a wooden skewer inserted into the center of the cake comes out with just a little chocolate sticking to it, 30 to 35 minutes or a bit longer.

Remove cake from the oven and run the tip of a small sharp knife around the top to release cake from the sides of pan. The cake will fall to about half the height of the pan as it cools, and the top may be crusty and cracked in many places. When completely cool, remove the side of the pan. (If not ready to serve, wrap the cake and pan in plastic wrap and let stand overnight at room temperature. You can also refrigerate the cake and serve it cold.) Cover the cake with a wire rack and invert. Remove pan bottom and paper; cover cake with another rack and invert again. With a large metal spatula, slide cake onto a cake plate.

To serve, rinse a knife in hot water and shake off excess water before making each cut. Cut into thin wedges, and pass the Crème Anglaise or Crème Chantilly separately.

SOUFFLÉ "ROULADE" AU CHOCOLAT AMER
Bittersweet Chocolate Roulade Soufflé

SERVES 8 TO 10

Here's a soufflé that's really a baked ganache—chocolate melted in heavy cream that has been heated—with beaten egg whites folded in. The roulade is so light it melts in your mouth. After baking in a standard-size jelly-roll pan, you let the cake cool completely, then lift it out of the pan by its parchment lining. After spreading with the whipped cream praline, you use the parchment to help roll the cake around the filling. And that's it! Transfer the cake to a board or platter, dust lightly with unsweetened cocoa, and cut into serving slices. The flavor of this cake is very bittersweet. If you prefer a less assertive chocolate flavor, substitute semisweet chocolate.

Serve with some fresh berries alongside each portion—and, if you wish, some Crème Anglaise or Crème Chantilly.

Roulade

Unsalted butter, for pan

3 to 4 tablespoons unsweetened cocoa, for baking
   pan

$^3/_4$ cup heavy cream

6 ounces bittersweet chocolate, chopped

6 large egg whites ($^3/_4$ cup), room temperature

$^1/_4$ teaspoon cream of tartar

$1^1/_2$ tablespoons granulated sugar

Unsweetened cocoa powder, for garnish

Whipped Cream Praline Filling

$^3/_4$ cup heavy cream

$^1/_2$ teaspoon vanilla extract

1 tablespoon Cognac or orange liqueur (optional)

1 tablespoon confectioners' sugar

3–4 tablespoons pulverized Praline aux Amandes
   (page 117)

Crème Anglaise (page 114) or Crème Chantilly
   (page 115), for serving (optional)

Adjust an oven rack to the center position and preheat the oven to 350 degrees F. Butter a $15^1/_2$ x $10^1/_2$ x 1-inch jelly-roll pan. Line the pan with cooking parchment, allowing excess parchment to extend an inch or two above the sides. Butter the parchment and dust bottom of pan lightly with unsweetened cocoa. Knock out excess.

For the roulade, heat the cream in a small heavy saucepan over medium heat until scalding hot, a point just before it boils. Remove pan from the heat and add the chocolate. Wait 1 minute, then stir with a whisk until the chocolate is melted and ganache is completely smooth. Cool until tepid.

Beat the egg whites on medium speed until foamy and then add the cream of tartar. Continue beating until whites form soft peaks. Add the granulated sugar and beat a minute or so more,

continued >

until whites form stiff, shiny peaks. Stir one-fourth of the egg whites into the ganache, then fold ganache into remaining whites only until no whites show.

Spread the soufflé batter in prepared pan and bake 10 minutes. The roulade should be puffy and light and a toothpick inserted into the center should come out clean. It's important that the roulade be completely cooked, but it's also important that it not be overbaked or rolling it around the filling later will be difficult. Cool completely in its pan, an hour or longer.

For the filling, whip the cream in a chilled bowl with chilled beaters until cream begins to thicken. Add the vanilla, liqueur (if using), and confectioners' sugar; continue beating until the cream holds a soft shape. Do not beat until stiff. Fold in the praline.

Remove the cooled roulade from the baking pan holding the parchment extensions, and set it on the countertop with a long side facing you. Spread the filling evenly on the roulade, going almost to the edges.

Lift the long side of roulade nearest you by the parchment, and fold about 2 inches of it onto the filling. Don't be concerned about the roulade breaking. Carefully peel back a few inches of the parchment, and continue rolling the roulade over the filling until you've formed a log with seam side down. The parchment should peel away easily from the roulade.

If not ready to serve, leave the roulade enclosed in parchment. Transfer the roulade carefully to a board or platter and refrigerate.

When ready to serve, remove parchment from the roulade. Dust lightly with unsweetened cocoa powder, cut into diagonal slices and serve on dessert plates.

SOUFFLÉ D'ILES FLOTTANTES À LA PRALINE
Almond Praline Soufflé Floating Islands

SERVES 6

Here's a perfect light and airy dessert for just about anytime. You beat egg whites with sugar to make a meringue and fold in a homemade powdered almond praline. After baking the soufflé in a hot water bath and letting it cool, you upend it onto a platter, cut it into portions, and float each on chilled Crème Anglaise. Make the Praline aux Amandes, Crème Anglaise and Coulis aux Framboises up to 3 days ahead. You can also make the soufflé a day ahead and refrigerate it. When you want to serve, it will only take a few minutes.

Unsalted butter for mold

10 tablespoons superfine sugar (also called baker's sugar) or granulated sugar, plus 2–3 tablespoons more for mold

8 large egg whites (1 cup), room temperature

Pinch of salt

$^1/_2$ teaspoon cream of tartar

1 teaspoon vanilla extract

$^1/_2$ cup pulverized Praline aux Amandes (page 117)

Crème Anglaise (page 114)

Coulis aux Framboises (page 119)

Adjust an oven rack to the lower third position and preheat the oven to 350 degrees F. Butter an 8-cup soufflé pan thoroughly (a French charlotte mold is ideal; the one I use is 4 inches tall by 7$^1/_4$ inches across the top), right up to the rim. Add 2 to 3 tablespoons sugar and then tip and turn the pan to coat well with the sugar. Knock out excess sugar.

The soufflé must be baked in a water bath. Have ready a roasting pan with sides about 3 inches high. Bring several quarts water to the boil and keep hot to pour into the roasting pan just before baking.

In the bowl of a stand mixer, beat the egg whites and a pinch of salt on medium speed for about 1 minute, just until the whites turn frothy. Add cream of tartar and beat until whites form soft peaks when the beater is raised. Still on medium speed, gradually beat in the 10 tablespoons sugar, waiting about 10 seconds between additions. Increase speed to medium-high and beat until the whites form stiff, shiny, unwavering peaks when the beater is raised. Beat in the vanilla. Fold in the praline powder and spoon the meringue into prepared mold, packing it in. The pan will be almost full.

Put the soufflé pan into the roasting pan and add boiling water to reach halfway up the sides of soufflé pan. Bake 35 to 40 minutes, until a wooden skewer inserted into the center comes out clean. During baking the soufflé may rise several inches above the rim.

Remove soufflé pan from its water bath and set on a rack to cool. The soufflé will sink to about half the height of its mold. When completely cool, cover the soufflé pan with a dessert platter and invert the two. The soufflé should fall out easily. Cover the soufflé with an inverted bowl until ready to serve. Or refrigerate for no more than 1 day.

To serve, cut the soufflé into 6 portions. Divide the Crème Anglaise among six dessert plates or bowls. Set portions of the soufflé onto the dessert dishes, drizzle with the coulis, and serve.

SOUFFLÉ FROID AU FRUIT DE LA PASSIFLORE
Cold Passion Fruit Soufflé

SERVES 8

Cold soufflés are more properly called mousses. But if you pour the batter laced with gelatin into a soufflé mold surrounded with a paper collar, the soufflé rises above the rim of the mold. When you peel away the paper after the soufflé has set, you have the illusion of a dessert that has puffed in the oven.

Passion fruit purée adds its own exotic and special fruitiness to this soufflé. It's a tropical fruit that has gained great popularity over the decades in pavlova, a meringue dessert from Australia and New Zealand.

Passion Fruit Custard

$^3/_4$ cup passion fruit juice

1 envelope plus $^1/_2$ teaspoon unflavored gelatin

Finely grated zest of 2 oranges (about 2 packed tablespoons)

1 cup plus 1 tablespoon granulated sugar, divided

$1^1/_2$ cups whole milk

8 large egg yolks

For the Soufflé

6 large egg whites ($^3/_4$ cup), room temperature

$^1/_4$ teaspoon cream of tartar

2 tablespoons granulated sugar

$^3/_4$ cup heavy cream, plus more for serving (optional)

Seasonal fresh fruits (optional)

You'll need a 5- to 6-cup soufflé mold about 3 inches tall, and a bath of ice and water to chill the custard.

To prepare the mold, cut a 2-foot length of wax paper and fold it in half lengthwise. Wrap the wax paper around the mold to overlap slightly, and secure it with a piece or two of Scotch tape. Wrap kitchen twine tightly around the collar to make sure the filling will not leak. The collar should extend from the base of the mold to a few inches above it. Set the prepared mold on a plate.

For the custard, combine the juice and gelatin in a small bowl and let stand at least 10 minutes for the gelatin to soften.

Mash the zest with 1 tablespoon of the sugar in a mortar with a pestle or in a small bowl with a wooden spoon to extract the orange oil flavor. Scrape zest into a 3-quart saucepan and add the milk. Set pan over medium heat and bring milk to the boil, stirring occasionally, to dissolve the sugar.

continued >

Beat the egg yolks in a medium bowl with a wire whip or on medium speed with an electric mixer until they are well combined. Gradually add the 1 cup of sugar, beating constantly for 3 to 4 minutes, until the yolks become thick and pale and form a ribbon when the beater is raised.

Beat in the hot milk a teaspoon or so at a time, very gradually at first. Add milk more rapidly after about half of it has been mixed into the yolks. Pour the custard into the saucepan used to heat the milk. Set the pan over medium heat and cook, stirring constantly with a heatproof rubber spatula, making sure to go all over the bottom and around sides of the pan. You are making a custard sauce like crème anglaise. This will take several minutes, and you must make sure the sauce never reaches the boil or the egg yolks will curdle. Lift the pan off the heat occasionally if you feel the custard is heating too quickly. The custard should coat the spatula with a thin film, and when you swipe it with a finger, the path should remain. The custard temperature should register between 175 and 180 degrees F.

As soon as the custard is cooked, take pan off the heat and immediately add the softened gelatin. Stir for 1 to 2 minutes to make sure the gelatin is dissolved.

Set the saucepan into a pan with ice and water and stir with a spatula to begin cooling the hot custard. Continue stirring until the custard feels just warm to the fingertip. Remove pan from water bath.

For the soufflé, in a large, clean bowl with clean beaters, whip egg whites until foamy, about 1 minute. Add cream of tartar and beat until the whites form soft peaks. Gradually beat in 2 tablespoons sugar until the whites form stiff, shiny peaks. Give the tepid custard sauce a stir, and fold in about half of the beaten whites. Fold in remaining whites, and keep folding gently to maintain as much of the air as possible.

When the custard and whites just feel cool to the fingertip, whip the ¾ cup cream in a chilled bowl with chilled beaters only until the cream is barely thick and holds a soft shape, what the French call *crème chantilly*. Add cream to the custard and fold together gently.

Pour into prepared mold and refrigerate for 4 to 6 hours to set the soufflé. Drape a piece of plastic wrap loosely on top of the wax paper collar to prevent the soufflé from drying out. You can make this dessert a day ahead.

To serve, remove the paper collar and set the soufflé on a dessert platter. Bring to the table. Use large spoons to serve portions, and accompany with in-season fresh fruits and more crème chantilly if desired.

Soufflé Glacé aux Framboises
Frozen Raspberry Soufflé

SERVES 12 OR MORE

This is a spectacular dessert for a special occasion. The soufflé mixture fills an 8-cup soufflé mold and reaches to the top of a high paper collar. After freezing it, you peel away the collar to reveal a soufflé that appears to have risen several inches above the rim of the mold. Breathtaking! Serve with cold raspberry sauce.

Raspberry Purée

4 cups (1¼ pounds) fresh raspberries, plus 1½ cups more for decorating and serving

¼ cup sugar

2 tablespoons fresh lemon juice

2 tablespoons framboise (raspberry liqueur)

Italian Meringue

2 cups sugar

1 cup water

10 large egg whites (about 1¼ cups), room temperature

½ teaspoon cream of tartar

Finishing the Soufflé

2 cups heavy cream

Raspberry Sauce

Reserved raspberry purée

¼ cup sugar

2 tablespoons framboise or Kirsch (optional)

1 cup fresh raspberries

You'll need an 8-cup porcelain or glass mold. Tear a sheet of wax paper long enough to wrap around the mold with about 3 inches of overlap. Fold the paper in half lengthwise. Brush a thin layer of tasteless vegetable oil onto one side of the wax paper (just the top portion that faces inward and extends above the rim of the mold) and secure it to the mold with tape, making sure there's no gap between the rim of the mold and the paper. Wrap kitchen twine tightly around the collar to make sure the filling will not leak.

Purée 4 cups raspberries in a food processor and pass through a fine strainer to remove the seeds. Measure 1 cup purée for the soufflé and transfer to a small bowl. Reserve remaining purée, covered in the refrigerator. Add the sugar, lemon juice, and framboise to the 1 cup purée and stir until sugar is dissolved.

continued >

For the Italian meringue, stir the sugar and water together in a medium heavy saucepan. Set pan over medium heat and stir occasionally until sugar is completely dissolved. Bring liquid to the boil over medium-high heat without stirring, cover pan, and cook 3 minutes; steam will wash down any sugar crystal that may have formed on the sides. Uncover pan and attach a candy/deep-fry thermometer. Cook without stirring until the liquid registers 240 degrees F. The syrup will be a pale amber color.

Start beating the egg whites as soon as you cover the pan for the syrup's 3-minute cooking. Using a stand mixer with a whip attachment, beat the egg whites on medium speed until frothy, about 1 minute. Add cream of tartar and beat on medium to medium-high speed until whites are glossy and form firm peaks when the beater is raised. This may take 2 to 3 minutes. Do not over-beat. Let whites stand.

When the syrup reaches 240 degrees F, immediately start beating the egg whites again on medium speed and, holding the syrup pan about 8 inches above the mixing bowl, drizzle hot syrup into the egg whites in a slow, steady stream. Be very careful not to rush this step or you risk cooking the whites. Once all the syrup has been added (just pour what will come out of the saucepan, don't scrape the pan), increase the mixer speed to medium-high and beat until meringue has risen almost to the top of the bowl and has cooled to barely tepid. This step can take 15 minutes or more but is crucial to the success of the recipe.

Scrape the meringue into a large, wide mixing bowl—stainless steel or whatever you have on hand. Fold the raspberry purée into the meringue until it is an even pink color with no white streaks.

In a clean chilled bowl with a clean whip attachment, beat the heavy cream until it holds a firm shape but is not completely stiff. Carefully fold cream into the raspberry meringue until thoroughly combined. Scrape soufflé into prepared mold and smooth the top. The soufflé may reach right to the top of the paper collar. Set soufflé dish on a tray and freeze for at least 6 hours, preferably overnight. When soufflé is frozen solid, lay a piece of plastic wrap loosely over the top.

When ready to serve, prepare the Raspberry Sauce. Stir the sugar and liqueur, if using, into reserved raspberry purée until sugar is dissolved; stir in raspberries. Keep cold until serving time. Remove paper collar from the soufflé mold and set soufflé on a dessert platter. A doily under the soufflé is a nice touch. Score the top of soufflé a good 1/4 inch deep in a wide crosshatch pattern. Decorate top of soufflé with fresh raspberries and bring dessert to the table.

To serve, use a sharp knife to cut portions going down to the rim of the soufflé dish, then cut into the soufflé horizontally to release the portions. Cut remaining soufflé into portions in the pan. Or dip the soufflé mold briefly into a pan of very hot water to release soufflé from sides of the mold, cover with a large plate, and invert the two. Lift off the mold and cut dessert into portions. Place servings on dessert plates and pass Raspberry Sauce separately. Any leftover soufflé can be left in its mold, covered, and stored in the freezer for up to 3 days.

SOUFFLÉS GLACÉS AUX FRAISES
Frozen Strawberry Soufflés

SERVES 8

This dessert will remind you of very smooth strawberry ice cream. Make these party-perfect, pink-colored soufflés when strawberries are ripe and juicy and at their peak of flavor. I like to pass the puréed fruit through a fine strainer to remove the seeds, but this is entirely up to you. When serving these to children, substitute orange juice for the liqueur. If you have some egg whites in the freezer, this recipe is an opportunity to use them.

You'll be making sugar syrup to beat into the whites and creating an Italian meringue. At sea level, cook the syrup to 236 degrees F. For every 500-foot gain in altitude, subtract 1 degree Fahrenheit. The desserts may be made 2 to 3 days ahead. When completely frozen, cover the tops of the collars with a sheet of plastic wrap or aluminum foil.

1 pound (2 pints) fresh strawberries, stemmed and hulled	1 cup sugar
	$^1/_2$ cup water
2 tablespoons Grand Marnier, Kirsch or orange juice	1 cup heavy whipping cream
4 large egg whites ($^1/_2$ cup), room temperature	$^1/_4$ cup confectioners' sugar
Pinch of salt	1 teaspoon vanilla extract
$^1/_4$ teaspoon cream of tartar	

Cut 8 strips of wax paper or foil that measure 13 x 4 inches and wrap tightly around eight 4-ounce soufflé ramekins, taping collars in place. Set prepared molds on a baking sheet.

Purée the berries in a food processor for about 1 minute, or until liquefied. Stop occasionally to scrape sides of the work bowl. Pass purée through a fine strainer to remove the tiny seeds. You'll have 1$^1/_2$ cups of purée. (If you decide to skip this step, you'll have slightly more purée.) Stir in the liqueur and refrigerate.

Using a stand mixer with a whip attachment, beat the egg whites with salt on medium speed until frothy, about 1 minute. Add cream of tartar and beat until whites are glossy and form firm peaks when the beater is raised. Do not overbeat. The whites will hold perfectly well while you prepare the sugar syrup.

Put sugar into a small (1-quart) heavy saucepan and add the water. Do not stir. Set pan over medium heat and bring to the boil, swirling pan occasionally by its handle. When sugar is dissolved and the liquid looks clear and is at the boil, cover pan and boil for 3 minutes to wash down any sugar crystals that may have formed on the sides. Uncover pan and continue boiling until the syrup registers 236 degrees F on a candy or digital thermometer. (This is known as the soft-ball stage. If testing without a thermometer, drizzle a few drops of hot syrup into cold water and reach in with your fingers to feel the cooled syrup; it will feel soft when you squish it.)

Immediately start beating the egg whites again on medium speed and, holding the syrup pan about 8 inches above the mixing bowl, drizzle hot syrup into the egg whites in a slow, steady stream. Once all the syrup has been added—just pour what will come out of the saucepan, don't scrape the pan—increase speed to medium-high and continue beating until the meringue forms stiff peaks and feels cool to the touch.

In another bowl, with chilled beaters, whip the cream, confectioners' sugar and vanilla on medium speed until the cream holds a soft shape. Do not beat the cream stiff.

Transfer meringue to a large bowl and gradually fold in the strawberry purée with a large rubber spatula. If the meringue looks lumpy at any point, shift to a whisk to complete the folding. Fold in the softly whipped cream.

Divide the strawberry meringue among prepared soufflé dishes using a generous 1 cup for each mold. Don't bother smoothing the tops. Freeze until firm, at least 4 hours.

Remove the collars. Allow soufflés to stand about 10 minutes before serving.

CHAPTER 4

RECETTES DE BASE
Basic Recipes

This chapter includes several basic recipes that you will want to make a part of your standard culinary repertoire and are sure to use again and again. Some of these recipes are components of my soufflés, while others are accompaniments to them, but all are adaptable and serve many other delicious purposes.

CRÈME ANGLAISE
Custard Sauce

MAKES ABOUT 2 1/2 CUPS

This classic custard sauce is one of the most versatile around. It is excellent served with dessert soufflés, poured over crumbles or crisps, spooned alongside chocolate cake or brownies, or drizzled onto fresh strawberries or peaches. The flavor of the sauce can be varied by adding different liqueurs and spirits, such as Grand Marnier, Kahlua, Cognac, dark rum, amaretto, Frangelico, Chambord, or whatever else grabs your fancy. And you can increase the sauce's richness by using all half-and-half and adding an extra egg yolk.

2 cups whole milk, or 1 cup whole milk and 1 cup
   half-and-half
1 vanilla bean or 2 teaspoons vanilla extract

5 large egg yolks
Pinch of salt
1/2 cup sugar

Put the milk, or milk and half-and-half, in a medium heavy saucepan. If using a vanilla bean, split it lengthwise, scrape the seeds into the milk, and add the pod. (If using vanilla extract, reserve it until the sauce has been cooked.) Heat slowly to a simmer and then turn off heat and let the vanilla steep for about 30 minutes. Remove the pod. Wash and dry it for another use (such as burying it in a jar of granulated sugar to make vanilla sugar).

Reheat vanilla milk over medium heat until bubbling but not boiling; keep warm.

Whisk the yolks and a pinch of salt well in a medium bowl until slightly thickened, about 1 minute. Gradually whisk in the sugar. Whisk in the hot milk about 1 tablespoon at a time. When about half the milk has been added, whisk in the remainder in larger additions. Transfer the liquid back into the saucepan and set the pan over medium heat. Cook, stirring constantly with a heat-proof rubber spatula, until you see wisps of steam rising from the surface and the liquid has thickened slightly, about 8 minutes. The liquid should coat the spatula with a thin film and when you swipe a fingertip through the film a path should remain. The temperature of the Crème Anglaise should be between 175 and 180 degrees F. Do not allow the liquid to boil or the yolks will curdle. Pass the Crème Anglaise through a fine strainer and stir in the vanilla if using. Cool to room temperature, then cover and refrigerate until very cold. (Can be prepared 4 to 5 days ahead.)

CRÈME CHANTILLY
Whipped Cream
MAKES 3 CUPS

The French tend to whip cream to a thickness that barely leaves traces of the whisk in the cream. This is known as Crème Chantilly. At this stage, the cream is airy and light and pairs well with all sorts of soufflés. Of course, it also goes splendidly with just about anything sweet that would be made even more delicious with a whipped cream garnish, whether fresh berries, cake or pie. You can flavor the cream any way you like; a tablespoon or so of liqueur is always a nice addition.

$1^1/_2$ cups heavy cream, chilled

1 teaspoon vanilla extract

1 tablespoon liqueur of your choice, optional

Confectioners' sugar

Put the cream into a medium bowl and set it into a larger bowl filled with ice and water. Whisk cream until it begins to thicken. Add the vanilla, liqueur, if using, and sugar to taste and continue whisking only until the cream thickens to the point where you can see traces of the whisk pattern. Cream should double in volume. Refrigerate until ready to use. Whisk it a few times just before serving.

CRÊPES

MAKES 12 LARGE (7½-INCH) OR 18 TO 24 SMALL (5-INCH) CRÊPES

Oh, the wonder of crêpes. They are delicious on their own, with butter and sugar, with jam or Nutella, or rolled around a myriad of ingredients both sweet and savory. And surprise, surprise, they are fabulous wrapped around soufflés. Just remember that the batter needs to rest at least an hour—or up to one day— before you use it, so plan accordingly.

1½ cups whole milk, plus more if needed

3 large eggs

1½ cups (6¾ ounces) all-purpose flour

2 tablespoons sugar

⅛ teaspoon salt

¼ cup melted unsalted butter, cooled, plus more for cooking crêpes

Put the milk, eggs, flour, sugar, salt, and ¼ cup melted butter into a blender jar and mix on low speed for 15 seconds. Scrape the jar to dislodge any flour and blend on high speed until completely smooth, about 30 seconds. (Alternatively, if making by hand, whisk the milk and eggs together in a large bowl. Add the flour gradually, whisking. Then whisk in the sugar and salt until very smooth. Whisk in the ¼ cup melted butter.) Strain batter through a fine-mesh sieve into a medium bowl. Cover, and refrigerate at least 1 hour or overnight.

When ready to make crêpes, whisk the batter well, then adjust consistency, if necessary, by adding more milk; batter should be thin. Ladle or spoon a scant ¼ cup batter into a dry ¼ cup measure and set aside.

Brush a 7- to 8-inch nonstick skillet or crêpe pan lightly with melted butter and set the pan over medium-high heat. When hot, lift the pan by its handle, tilting the lip of the pan away from you. Pour batter onto the far end of the pan, then lift and rotate pan in all directions to make a crêpe that covers the bottom of the pan. Set the pan back down on the burner. If any gaps remain in the crêpe, you can always fill them in with drops of batter. Cook until the crêpe has a lacy edge that looks dry and turns a light brown, 30 to 45 seconds. Working quickly, loosen the edges of the crêpe with a metal spatula going all around the pan, lift up a far end of the crêpe with your fingers, and flip it over towards you. Cook a few seconds more on the second side then slide the crêpe onto a plate. The original bottom of the crêpe, the side facing you, should be nicely browned. The first crêpe or two are always tests to judge the heat and batter consistency. You have more than enough batter for any mistakes.

Continue making crêpes—no need to butter the pan after the first crêpe—and stacking them on top of each other until all the batter is used. Cover with plastic wrap and refrigerate. (Can be prepared 1 to 2 days ahead, wrapped and refrigerated, or frozen up to 1 month.)

Praline aux Amandes
Almond Praline

MAKES 1 1/2 CUPS

This crunchy confection is delicious on its own, crumbled over ice cream, dusted over whipped cream, or folded into soufflés. The praline is also scrumptious made with hazelnuts, which need to be toasted and husked before using. Why not whip up a batch, put it in a beautiful jar and offer it up as a hostess gift or a holiday treat?

1 cup sugar
1 cup whole almonds, unblanched or blanched

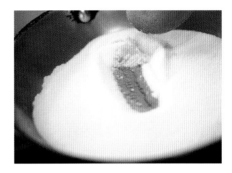

Oil a large baking sheet or marble pastry surface. Put the sugar into a 10-inch heavy skillet (do not use non-stick; you want to see the color of the caramel) and set over medium heat. Let the sugar cook undisturbed until it begins to melt, about 5 minutes; do not stir the sugar or move the skillet. Continue cooking the sugar, stirring occasionally, until it has melted completely and turns a deep caramel color, 1 to 2 minutes. Using the handle, swirl the skillet until the caramel begins to foam up, then remove skillet from the heat. (You may notice wisps of smoke coming from the caramel; do not be alarmed.) Immediately stir the almonds into the caramel. Pour the praline onto the prepared baking sheet or marble and leave it alone until it has cooled and hardened into a brittle.

Dislodge the brittle and break it up into chunks. Transfer chunks to a food processor and pulse to a powder; do not over-process or the powder will turn into a paste. Store praline in airtight container in the refrigerator. (Can be prepared up to a few weeks ahead or frozen up to 6 months. Bring to room temperature before using.)

CRÈME DE CITRON
Lemon Curd

MAKES 1 CUP

This citrus cream is excellent when mixed with Crème Anglaise or Crème Chantilly. Serve either concoction over fresh fruit, berry desserts or even French toast! The curd is fabulous as a filling for tarts, cakes and cookies, or as a swirl for vanilla ice cream. Or try it on its own, slathered on toast, English muffins or scones, or just eaten from a spoon.

5 large egg yolks

Pinch of salt

1/2 cup sugar

1/3 cup fresh lemon juice

1 tablespoon finely grated lemon zest

Whisk the yolks and salt together in a medium bowl. Gradually add the sugar, whisking until yolks become thick and pale. Whisk in the lemon juice and zest.

Transfer the yolks to a 1-quart heavy nonreactive saucepan and set over medium-low heat. Stir constantly with a heatproof rubber spatula until the curd has become a thick cream, 5 to 8 minutes; do not boil. The temperature should be between 180 and 185 degrees F.

Pass the curd through a strainer into a small bowl. Cool to room temperature. Cover tightly and refrigerate. (Can be prepared 1 week ahead.)

Coulis aux Framboises
Raspberry Coulis

MAKES ABOUT 1½ CUPS

This is a wonderful sauce to have on hand to serve over soufflés, ice cream, fresh fruit and absolutely anything chocolate. The color is spectacular!

½ cup sugar

¼ cup water

4 cups (1¼ pounds) fresh raspberries

1 teaspoon vanilla extract

1 tablespoon Framboise or Kirsch, optional

Stir the sugar and water together in a medium heavy saucepan over medium heat. Bring to the boil, then reduce heat to low and simmer 5 minutes. Add the raspberries and cook until berries are soft, 2 to 3 minutes. Pour berries into a blender jar and purée about 1 minute. Pass purée through a fine-mesh strainer, pressing on the fruit to extract as much of the pulp as possible. Stir in the vanilla and liqueur, if desired. Cover and refrigerate. (Can be prepared up to 4 days ahead.)

SAUCE AU CHOCOLAT
Chocolate Sauce

MAKES 1½ CUPS

This quick and easy bittersweet chocolate sauce is luscious poured over soufflés or ice cream. To serve with a soufflé, make a hole in the center of the soufflé and pour in a tablespoon or two of the sauce.

³/₄ cup unsweetened cocoa powder, preferably
    Dutch-process, strained to remove lumps
¹/₄ cup firmly packed light brown sugar, strained to
    remove lumps
¹/₂ cup sugar
Pinch of salt
1 cup water, divided
1 ounce bittersweet chocolate, chopped
2 tablespoons unsalted butter
1 teaspoon vanilla extract

Whisk together the cocoa, both sugars, and salt in medium heavy saucepan. Whisk in ¹/₃ cup water until smooth, then whisk in remaining water. Bring sauce to the boil over medium-high heat, stirring with a wooden spoon. Reduce heat to medium-low and simmer for 3 minutes, stirring occasionally. Remove from heat and whisk in the chopped chocolate, butter, and vanilla until smooth. Cool to room temperature, cover and refrigerate. Reheat briefly before serving, if desired. (Can be prepared 2 to 3 weeks ahead.)

Sauce au Tomate
Tomato Sauce

MAKES ABOUT 2¹/₂ CUPS

Here's a chunky all-purpose tomato sauce with Mediterranean flavors that is perfect alongside hot vegetable soufflés. It is also a great pasta sauce or addition to ragus or braised dishes. If you prefer a smooth sauce, purée in a food processor or blender.

3 tablespoons olive oil

1 cup finely chopped yellow onion

1 tablespoon finely chopped garlic

1 bay leaf

2 pounds Roma tomatoes, peeled, seeded and chopped

¹/₄ cup chopped fresh basil

¹/₄ cup chopped flat-leaf parsley

¹/₂ teaspoon salt

¹/₄ teaspoon sugar

¹/₄ teaspoon fennel seeds, crushed

¹/₄ teaspoon ground coriander seed

¹/₄ teaspoon freshly ground pepper

¹/₄ teaspoon cayenne pepper

Pinch of saffron, crumbled

Heat the oil in a 3-quart heavy saucepan over medium-low heat. Add the onion and cook until tender but not browned, stirring occasionally, 5 to 8 minutes. Add the garlic and bay leaf and cook 2 minutes, stirring constantly. Stir in the tomatoes and all remaining ingredients. Increase heat to medium and bring to a simmer. Reduce heat to low and cook, stirring occasionally, until sauce is thick enough to hold a soft shape in a spoon, about 30 minutes. Taste and adjust seasonings. Serve hot or at room temperature. (Can be prepared 3 to 4 days ahead. Cool, cover and refrigerate. Or freeze up to 2 months.)

About the Author

Greg Patent is the winner of the James Beard Award for his cookbook *Baking in America*. His book *A Baker's Odyssey* won the Cordon d'Or Award. Greg has written for all the major food magazines, and for thirteen years was a contributor to *Cooking Light* magazine. He writes about food regularly for his local newspaper, the *Missoulian*, and *Missoula Magazine*, and co-hosts a weekly Montana Public Radio show about food, *The Food Guys*. He writes a blog, *www.thebakingwizard.com,* and you can follow him on Twitter and Facebook. He lives in Missoula, Montana, with his wife, Dorothy.

ACKNOWLEDGMENTS

Writing and shaping a cookbook is never a solitary affair, and I want to thank my editor, Madge Baird, for her constant guidance and encouragement; my friend Lisa Yockelson for supporting my work over many years; Kelly Gorham, my photographer, for his keen eye and perseverance; Kimberlee Carlson, for her imaginative styling of each soufflé; Susan Talbot, for loaning us some of her treasured French kitchen equipment; and my wife, Dorothy, for her unfailing good taste.

RECIPES BY CHAPTER

METRIC CONVERSION CHART

Volume Measurements

U.S.	Metric
1 teaspoon	5 ml
1 tablespoon	15 ml
1/4 cup	60 ml
1/3 cup	75 ml
1/2 cup	125 ml
2/3 cup	150 ml
3/4 cup	175 ml
1 cup	250 ml

Weight Measurements

U.S.	Metric
1/2 ounce	15 g
1 ounce	30 g
3 ounces	90 g
4 ounces	115 g
8 ounces	225 g
12 ounces	350 g
1 pound	450 g
2 1/4 pounds	1 kg

Temperature Conversion

Fahrenheit	Celsius
250	120
300	150
325	160
350	180
375	190
400	200
425	220
450	230

INDEX